Pollinator Gardening
for the South

Pollinator Gardening
for the South

Creating Sustainable Habitats

DANESHA SETH CARLEY & ANNE M. SPAFFORD

THE UNIVERSITY OF NORTH CAROLINA PRESS *Chapel Hill*

*The production of this book was
supported by a generous grant from the
Center for Integrated Pest Management
at North Carolina State University.*

*Promotion of this book was supported in
part by a generous gift from Duke Energy.*

Cover photo © Danesha Seth Carley

Stock art: notepaper © iStock/Nic_Taylor; wildflowers
© iStock/Val_Iva; honey bee © iStock/Olga Nefedova;
dragonfly © iStock/Ievgeniia Lytvynovych; ant © iStock/
SergeyDolinin; lady beetle © iStock/retrofutur

Library of Congress Cataloging-in-Publication Data
Names: Carley, Danesha Seth, 1976– author. |
Spafford, Anne, author.
Title: Pollinator gardening for the South: creating sustainable
habitats / Danesha Seth Carley and Anne Spafford.
Description: Chapel Hill: University of North Carolina Press,
[2020] | Includes index.
Identifiers: LCCN 2020024363 | ISBN 9781469659411
(paperback: alk. paper) | ISBN 9781469659428 (ebook)
Subjects: LCSH: Gardening to attract wildlife—Southern
States. | Pollinators. | Bees. | Gardens—Design.
Classification: LCC QL59 .C27 2020 | DDC 635.9—dc23
LC record available at https://lccn.loc.gov/2020024363

Contents

Acknowledgments, viii

Introduction, 1
The Southern Life of Bee Enthusiasts

Pollinators Make the World Go 'Round, 5

The Importance of Pollinators, 5
A Brief History Lesson on Managed Bees, 7
Bee Health: The Good, the Bad, and the Ugly, 10
Being a Good Bee Steward, 13
Get Ready to Dig In, 15

Butterflies, Bees & Beyond, 17

Non-Bee Pollinators, 17
Bees: Order Hymenoptera—Saving the Best for Last, 31
Pollinators Are Worth Protecting, 44

Pollination & Garden Design, 45
Where Science and Art Meet

How Plants Approach Pollination, 45
How Bees Approach Pollination, 51
Food and a Safe Place to Call Home, 53
Garden Design Basics, 55
Small Creatures, Complex Bee-havior, 70
One Size Does Not Fit All, 72

Designing a Habitat to Support Pollinators, 73

Garden Context: Considering Use and
   Experience, 74
Garden Placement, 74
It Helps to Be Prepared, 78
Tools of the Trade — So Many Plant Types!, 82
Beauty Alone Isn't Enough, 85
Planting Design Boot Camp, 86
Selecting Design Qualities for Your Garden, 101
A Garden for All Seasons, 101
Plant Selection, 105
Got Weeds? Good!, 112

Digging In, 113
Installation and Management

Before You Start, 113
Garden Bed Preparation, 115
Plant-Buying Options, 117
Proper Planting Times, 121
Planting Techniques, 122
Pollinator Habitat Management: If You Build It,
   They Will Come . . . but Then What?, 123
Time to Play in the Dirt, 127

Pollinator Gardening Big & Small, 129

No Yard? Plant a Container Garden, 129
The Parkway (or Devil Strip), 131
Pocket Gardens in Commercial and Communal
   Settings, 134
Health-Care Facilities, 135
Home Is Where the Bees Are, 135
Schools and College Campuses, 139
Greenways and Bike Trails, 143
The Garden as Art: A Museum Setting, 143
Botanical Gardens and Arboretums, 143
Golf Courses, 145
Be Bold, Be Brave, Be a Pollinator Champion, 147

Index, 149

Acknowledgments

WRITING A BOOK IS HARD. It is something that requires a great deal of time, focus, and, yes, coffee. It also requires confidence and, in this case, a great coauthor. This book would not have been possible without the encouragement, ideas, laughs, and hard work brought to this project by my amazing coauthor, Anne Spafford. She's not only a fellow coffee drinker and pollinator enthusiast, but also, a true friend.

I'm eternally grateful for the incredible and unwavering support of my parents, Linda and Craig Seth. Were it not for my unconventional and magical upbringing in the foothills of the Appalachian Mountains, among the Dutchman's breeches, trout lilies, and trillium, I would not have such heartfelt appreciation for nature, which I grew up dancing and singing in.

The period of my life while writing this book was filled with ups and downs. But my family, Minh, Tod, and Phil, never gave up on me. My dogs were always fed, and the laundry was (almost) always done. Sometimes it is those little things that allow the creative spirit to be free to create. Thank you each for supporting my need to feed that creative spirit and making it possible for me to embark on travels to wondrous places and to photograph the beautiful bees and flowers you see in this book.

Thanks to everyone who helped me get from start to finish on this book: Elaine Maisner, our super-positive editor; Jen O'Brien, Marisol Mata, and Lauren Kilpatrick, the inspiration for my newfound love of bees and buzzy things and the plants that support them; and Tom Rufty, my mentor and great friend, who never said no when

I wanted to share my favorite photos of flowers and flying insects with someone.

And finally, thank you, dear reader. I hope you enjoy this book as much as we have enjoyed writing it. I hope this book brings you inspiration, knowledge, and the desire to go outside and plant something to help us save the bees!

Danesha Carley

WRITING A BOOK TAKES a tremendous amount of energy and focus, aided by copious amounts of coffee and chocolate. I am thankful for all the pollinators who support life on this planet, but I am particularly indebted to those pollinators that make coffee and cocoa beans possible.

I am thankful that Danesha joined me on this wild journey. We have worked together on several habitat projects, but this book has been our most challenging and longest collaboration. I appreciate her knowledge of bees, but I am also incredibly thankful for her passion for pollinators (it's downright contagious), humor, and friendship. It is a true testament to our friendship and the respect we have for each other's areas of knowledge that we are not only still on speaking terms but looking forward to our next endeavor.

I am thankful for Dr. Wayne Buhler, for his support, guidance, mentorship, and overall fanfare, and for other pollinator specialists, notably Dr. Elsa Youngsteadt and Debbie Roos, who shared their expertise. Thank you to my students, who serve as endless inspiration and make me ever so grateful to have one of the best jobs on the planet.

They are all splendid, but a few, past and present, deserve recognition. These students go the extra mile to inspire and invigorate me, making me a better professor: Amalie Lyday, Cole Lee, Melissa Amoabeng, Adam DeRose, Hays Johnson, Paige Mager, and Thomas Jackson.

Many others provided unwavering support— my mom, Barbara Horne; my aunt, Martha Ferdinand; local notables Brie Arthur and Will Hooker; and of course, my "sanity historian," Thomas Brown.

Finally, thank you, readers! The fact that you picked up this book tells me that you are the kind of person who cares about the environment and protecting pollinators, and who is also interested in developing beautifully designed landscapes. So thank you for your passion and for all you will contribute to increasing and improving pollinator habitats.

Anne Spafford

Pollinator
Gardening
for the South

Introduction

The Southern Life of Bee Enthusiasts

The American South is a truly special place. Honestly, we would say this even if we were not sitting outside in February with temperatures in the mid-70s and the sweet scent of flowering apricot (*Prunus mume*) and saucer magnolia (*Magnolia × soulangeana*) wafting across the garden to us. With its rich history and unique plant life, including stately longleaf pines, Spanish moss–covered live oaks, and enormous multitrunked magnolias—not to mention the food: sweet tea, chicken and buttermilk waffles, drop biscuits with molasses, chicory coffee—the South is a special place. The South is our home; this is where our passions have rooted us. This is what we know best. We want to share our excitement and knowledge with you so that you learn to love pollinator gardening here in the South as much as we do.

We are horticulture professors and, of course, plant nerds. We are dedicated to beautifying and protecting green space in our urban environment. We are also bee nerds. We love plants *and* bees. And to be perfectly honest, butterflies, beetles, and even flies are pretty darn cool, too. In this book we want to share our love of plants, design, green space, and pollinators large and small with gardeners with all levels of experience. This book is for anyone with a few yards of patio or garden space, and curiosity and concern for the synergy between gardens and pollinators. It is for home gardeners and landscape professionals. It is for master gardeners and students of horticulture and landscape architecture. If you are not already a self-proclaimed plant, bee, and/or bug nerd, then keep reading so we can turn you into one.

It made sense for us to write a book that was focused on the South; one of us has lived in the South for over twenty years, and the other was born and raised in the South. We are southerners through and through. The South is in our blood. It is here in the South that we garden, raise our kids, and help shape future leaders in the fields of horticultural science and landscape architecture.

The reason we finally decided to take time away from our gardens and our classrooms to write a book was that, when searching for science-based recommendations for pollinator habitats, we found that most advice was based on anecdotes rather than grounded in science. As southerners who understand the importance of design and implementation based on evidence, we wanted to select plants that are proven to be good for pollinators and we wanted to protect bees and butterflies, beetles and flies. So we decided to write this book: it's the book we wanted to read. It will give you the most up-to-date information based on research-driven science and current thinking.

Often books and catalogs are disappointingly basic or too broad in their plant recommendations, so they do not provide appropriate recommendations for the Southeast (for example, they may recommend only sedums for green roofs, which are excellent for hot, dry locations—but the Southeast is also wet and humid, which isn't ideal for sedums, which prefer a much drier climate). One book may give wonderful advice for honey bees but neglect all the other bees; another may have beautiful photographs but provide precious little information on planting design strategies or even ideal plant choices; another may try to cover *only* native plants for *only* native bees in the whole great United States. (Whew, that was a lot to take in.) So

we've focused on the plants and pollinators commonly found in the South.

The South comes with its own set of challenges. It spans four USDA hardiness zones (eight if we include Florida). Throughout the year, the hottest states in the United States are concentrated in the South Central region and southeastern corner of the country. During every season, Florida, Louisiana, and Texas are consistently among the top four of the nation's hottest states, based on statewide average temperatures. Florida is the warmest state on average year-round, which is why it has its own hardiness zones. Annual precipitation amounts are on the rise, and rain tends to come in intermittent deluges, yet in the South we still experience droughts during our prime growing seasons. As we said, the South is a special case. Bless its heart.

This book, while appropriate for a scientific audience, will also appeal to concerned landscapers, home and hobby gardeners, and even entire garden clubs. Our goal is to take science from our classrooms into community halls and teach *everyone* enough science and practical knowledge that they too can become informed protectors of pollinators. Champions of green spaces. Bee garden gurus. When we say that anyone can be a pollinator champion and pollinator-friendly gardener, we mean you! No matter how small your garden plot or how large and unruly your yard, you can make a place for pollinators and help to save the bees (and butterflies, and flies, and beetles), one pollinator-friendly plant at a time.

Danesha, the scientist, is a sustainable urban ecologist, while Anne, the artist, is an experienced landscape designer. Together we have nearly five decades of experience. A scientist and an artist. We approach problem-solving differently, and our areas of expertise complement each other very well. We have designed and built numerous pollinator habitats together, and those gardens are better for having had both of our perspectives. This book, too, is better for having both our points of view. It's a perfect blend of art and science, with some pretty fabulous photos and ideas thrown in.

It is our hope that gardeners across our beautiful, biodiverse, history-rich, humid South will pick up our book and be inspired to get outside and select plants that both please humans and nourish pollinators. Anyone can be a pollinator gardener: all you need is the desire to garden and the willingness to get your hands dirty. So grab a glass of freshly squeezed lemonade, a big slice of hummingbird cake, and get ready to dig in.

Pollinators Make the World Go 'Round

With so many environmental problems challenging our planet, bad news and shocking headlines abound—so much so that it can feel overwhelming and it's hard to know what to tackle first. Many people want to help, to just do *something*, but they don't know how. It is not uncommon for homeowners and landscape professionals to come to us seeking advice on how to help the environment, especially when it comes to pollinator conservation and protection. The good news is that creating a pollinator-friendly garden or setting aside a bee-positive habitat is possible at any landscape scale, and we are here to help! But first, we need to set the stage by providing some important information about why everyone should plant a pollinator habitat. Much of this may be familiar to you, but some of it may not. Come with us as we cover the basics of why pollinators are important, some fun facts about different pollinators, and, finally, how you can plant a garden or create a habitat that is pollinator friendly.

The Importance of Pollinators

There are more than 250,000 species of flowering plants (angiosperms), and approximately 80 percent of these plants rely to some extent on almost as many species of animal pollinators to meet their reproductive needs. It is in large part due to this relationship that angiosperms were able to rapidly diversify between 90 million and 130 million years ago. This mutualism between flowering plants and insects such as bees, flies, and wasps is essential to the ecosystem. These critters carry pollen from plant to plant, which promotes outcrossing, aids in genetic recombination, and ensures sexual re-

The insects that pollinate plants are as diverse as the plants they pollinate. Here, clockwise from above, are a honey bee on a coneflower, a hoverfly on yarrow, and a male long-horned bee on a black-eyed Susan.

production in those plants (seed set, meaning the plants produce seed, and fruit set, the process in which flowers become fruit). The pollination of flowering plants also increases the aesthetic appeal of landscapes and contributes to wildlife habitats. Who doesn't enjoy seeing butterflies flitting lazily about a garden or bees buzzing busily from flower to flower?

In addition to contributing to beautiful landscapes, insect pollinators are responsible for contributing to the yield of 75 percent of the world's food crops. Put another way, between $235 billion and $577 billion worth of food relies on direct contributions by pollinators. While this is a great way to understand their importance if you are an economist, it may be easier to think of it this way: pollinators affect 35 percent of the world's crop production, increase yields of many leading food crops worldwide, and contribute to the making of many plant-derived medicines. Very broadly, one out of every three bites of food you eat is a result of some form of facilitated animal pollination.

We can thank pollinators for many of the bountiful crops we rely on, including blueberries, apples, pumpkins, brassicas (such as cabbage and broccoli), peppers, cantaloupes, squash, many beans, apricots, peaches, cherries, mangoes, grapes, olives, carrots, cucumbers, sunflower seeds, kiwis, lemons, various nuts, nutmeg, and tea. Think about the breakfast you ate today. Whole-grain toast with strawberry jam: thanks, bees. Orange juice: thanks, bees. Coffee with just a splash of cream: thanks, flies and bees. The coconut, raisins, and vanilla in your granola: thanks, flies and bees. And thanks, bees, for enhancing the output of the sustainably grown cotton used to make the shirt on

your back. We could go on and on, but you get the idea. Pollinators are of critical importance to our way of life.

A Brief History Lesson on Managed Bees

For over 3,500 years, humans have understood that bees and the pollination services they provide are important to agriculture. However, it was not until the mid-1700s that Joseph Gottlieb Kölreuter, a German professor of natural history, first demonstrated that insect visitation was a necessary for seed production in several economically important fruits, vegetables, and ornamental flowers. Once humans better understood the role of insect-aided pollination and subsequent fruit set, we were able to enhance crop productivity and exploit pollination for our own purposes, both on a small scale and commercially.

In general, only a few pollinator species are actively managed. Think of them as tiny livestock: kept in a box, kept in large quantities, bought and sold commercially, and moved from place to place seasonally. Of these, the darling of agriculture, *Apis mellifera*, the European honey bee (also called the western honey bee), is the most actively managed pollinator worldwide. Originally from Eurasia, it has been the primary managed pollinator throughout history, with records dating back to ancient Egypt. Managed honey bee colonies were later transported around the world and arrived in North America with European colonists in the 1600s. It was not until 1862 that modern apiculture was born in North America. L. L. Langstroth, a hobbyist beekeeper and minister in Philadelphia, origi-

Beekeepers actively manage honey bees in hives, which come in many sizes, colors, and styles. The boxlike hives shown here are traditional.

nated the concept of "confined bee space," a place where bees could be kept, moved, and managed. In fact, the Langstroth hive is named after L. L. Langstroth, who, in 1852, invented and subsequently patented his design. This hive has revolutionized modern beekeeping with its movable frame and top-bar hives, which let beekeepers safely manage the colonies and harvest honey without hurting the bees. This constructed creation and concept of managing bees ultimately allowed the large-scale commercial beekeeping and honey industry that exists today.

In the United States, honey bees are trucked around the entire country to overwinter in sunny southern climates such as Florida and then move north and west as demand dictates. Moving bees

is labor intensive and stressful for beekeepers and bees alike. In the spring, hundreds of hives wrapped in netting are packed onto tractor trailers, which typically carry between 400 and 500 hives each, secured with tie-downs, and sent on their way. They typically start in the South—first in citrus groves in Florida, then melon fields throughout the region, blueberry and caneberry (blackberries and raspberries) fields from Georgia to the Carolinas—and move north, to the apple orchards and fields of squash, cucumber, and pumpkin along the East Coast, and eventually up to cranberry bogs in Massachusetts and Maine.

Growers and farmers pay commercial beekeepers to place hives in blossoming fruit and vegetable fields in order to enhance crop yields, thereby making their farms more profitable. The service itself is not free; costs range from $10 to $180 per acre, depending on the number of hives, the season, the crop, and the weather. Apple producers in Virginia may pay around $65 per colony this year (2020), compared with $100 for pumpkin farmers in the same area. These "hives for hire" are used to pollinate more than one hundred commercially grown crops and are highly valued by farmers for their role as essential pollinators and by the hive owners for their production of wax and honey. In the South, in addition to honey bees, several species of bumblebees (*Bombus* spp.) are also actively managed, mainly for the pollination of greenhouse tomatoes. In 2012, managing honey bees and bumblebees for pollination services brought

Raspberry (left) and blueberry (right) plants both need bees to pollinate their flowers before they can set fruit.

in $655.6 million nationally, according to the U.S. Economic Research Service.

In addition to actively managing bees, there are other means of promoting pollinator communities. We can manipulate our environment to encourage species biodiversity and population growth. A term we first read about while doing research for this book was "passive management." This is a great way to describe what we are advocating in this book. Large-scale examples of passive management include planting wildflower strips along agricultural fields and roadways and increasing the number of flowering plants that produce pollen and/or nectar (also referred to as "floral resources") in yards and gardens. Smaller-scale examples include providing nest materials and nest sites and protecting nesting habitats in your yard. All these passive management strategies increase the abundance and diversity of the pollinator community.

The urban environment, in suburban neighborhoods or small garden plots within cities, has been shown to increase the abundance and diversity of bee communities because we gardeners tend to plant for seasonality and diversity in bloom size, shape, and color. Whereas in wild "natural" landscapes, such as parks and forests, there can be long periods of time when there are precious few floral resources, built gardens are often more ecologically productive because humans tend to choose plants that bloom throughout much of the year. British landscape ecologist James Hitchmough likens built gardens to all-night convenience stores for pollinators: they "stock" more food than would be available in a natural setting, twenty-four hours a day.

Bee Health: The Good, the Bad, and the Ugly

We have come a long way in our understanding of the benefits of bees since the first honey bee colonies were brought to America on ships from Europe in the 1600s, but there is still a great deal about bees we do not know. One question many people feel is extremely important is "Why are bees around the world dying?" And that is a really good question. Over the past few decades, insect pollinator populations have been declining around the globe. There are alarming numbers of honey bee deaths from accidental contact with inappropriately applied pesticides, overwintering hive deaths because hobbyist beekeepers lack the necessary experience and knowledge, and large-scale deaths in summer and winter associated with sudden colony collapses. Though scientists agree that populations of native bees—such as digger bees, squash bees, mason bees, and shaggy fuzzyfoot bees—also seem to be in decline, no one knows the extent of the decline because we have virtually no data on those populations to begin with.

Scientists know a lot more about the health of managed bee populations, most notably honey bees, than about wild native bees. Beekeepers keep a close eye on their hives, and it easier to count (or estimate) the numbers of live and dead bees in these hives. Honey bees, because they are social and managed, suffer from a number of maladies that are less likely to affect native (primarily nonsocial, or solitary) bees. In addition to the loss of habitat and foraging resources (shelter and food) because of increased urbanization and climate change, honey bees are especially susceptible to several pests and diseases. Many folks have heard of colony collapse disorder, but honey bees also face harmful insect pests, such as varroa mites, honey bee tracheal mites, and small hive beetles, and diseases, such as American foulbrood (a bacterial disease), chalkbrood (a fungus), and nosema (a spore-forming protozoa). While this list is not exhaustive by any means, these are the primary pests and diseases contributing to honey bee deaths.

Colony Collapse Disorder
Colony collapse disorder (CCD) is a syndrome specifically defined as a dead colony with no adult bees and with no dead bee bodies but with a live queen,

and usually honey and immature bees, still present. Colony collapse disorder occurs when a majority of the worker bees in a colony leave or "disappear" while the queen is left in the hive. Even with food and a few nurse bees left to care for the remaining immature bees and the queen, the hive cannot survive without the worker bees. These hives eventually die. During the winter of 2006–2007, the Environmental Protection Agency (EPA) reported that beekeepers were experiencing unusually high losses of between 30 and 90 percent of their hives. As many as 50 percent of these affected colonies demonstrated symptoms inconsistent with any known causes of honey bee death. The combination of events, bees leaving, queen starving, resulted in mass colony die-offs and was eventually called CCD. It was feared that this disorder would be the death of all honey bees nationwide.

It is difficult to sort through the multitude of reports and data that are available about colony losses, or the number of hives that do not survive over the winter months, which is considered the overall indicator for bee health. The EPA reported in 2015 that honey bee colony losses maintained an average of about 28.7 percent since 2006–2007 but dropped to 23.1 percent for the 2014–2015 winter. The number of those losses attributed to CCD dropped from roughly 60 percent of total hives lost in 2008 to 31.1 percent in 2013; in initial reports for 2014–2015 losses, CCD is not mentioned. More-recent numbers coming from the U.S. Department of Agriculture's Economics, Statistics, and Market Information System reported that honey bee colonies lost for "operations with five or more colonies" from January through March 2019 was around 15 percent, with the annual average loss in 2019 being right about 15 percent. In fact, the number of managed colonies that beekeepers have reported losing specifically from CCD has been waning since 2010, according to reports from the USDA's Agricultural Research Service.

The threat of CCD does seem to have abated, and scientists are turning their focus to other bee-health concerns. Perhaps that is one bullet dodged for bees.

Pesticides

There is a large and growing body of scientific evidence that some neonicotinoids (a class of insecticides used widely on farms and in urban landscapes; also called "neonics") can have both fatal and nonfatal effects on pollinators. Farmers and homeowners apply pesticides, fungicides, and herbicides to their crops and lawns to control insect pests, diseases, and weeds. Some of these chemicals, especially insecticides, are known to be highly toxic to bees, and when they come in direct contact with bees, they can cause sudden death.

However, bees can also be exposed to lingering chemical residues while visiting flowers. When they return to their colonies with the pesticide-laden pollen and/or nectar, they expose the other hive members. While exposure to smaller or diluted doses of chemicals may not directly kill bees, they may suffer a host of sublethal effects. Research, primarily in laboratories under very controlled conditions, shows that bees exposed to low doses of some pesticides will sometimes demonstrate learning deficits, impaired immune function, increased larval mortality, and shortened adult life span. It is thought that bees that are repeatedly exposed to small doses of these chemicals (as would happen when they frequently revisit flowers or crops that have been sprayed with pesticides) become more affected over time. The result of repeated small exposures is essentially a "depression" in the health of both individual bees and the overall population, as well as a potential increase in their susceptibility to other stressors.

To put this into perspective, consider your own health. When you are sleeping enough, eating mindfully, and staying comfortably active, in general, you are healthy. If your adorable eighteen-month-old niece sneezes cold germs directly into your face, your body's immune system can fight the germs, and you will still make it to that Saturday night card game. However, when your immune system is weakened because you're not getting enough sleep, you're eating peanut-butter-and-banana sandwiches while standing at the sink before running the kids to archery practice, and you're skipping that hot yoga class too often, you are far more likely to come down with a cold if you are exposed to toddler (or any other) germs.

The same is true with other animals as well. While you do not see bees at yoga (and if you do, they would probably prefer you let them back outside), bees can also get stressed out by poor nutrition, not enough rest, air pollution, overcrowding, and so on. When they are stressed out, their immune system is depressed, and they are more susceptible to diseases, pests, and pesticides.

Neonicotinoids are a systemic pesticide, which simply means these chemicals are actually absorbed by a plant when applied to its seeds, soil, or leaves. The chemicals then circulate through the plant's tissues, killing any insects that feed on them. However, it is likely that these chemicals (pesticides) are also found in plant nectar and pollen, allowing pollinators to be exposed to small doses while foraging on treated crops. A major criticism of the body of scientific research has been that most experiments investigating pollinator susceptibility to neonics have been conducted on honey bees under very controlled laboratory or simulated field conditions. Field studies tend to give us a better sense of what is happening "in the real world," and the only field study to date found that proximity to fields with neonic-coated seeds had no significant effect on honey bee colony health, though significant negative impacts on other bee populations, including bumblebee colonies, were reported.

The long and the short of it is that although low-level indirect exposures to neonics and other chemicals do not typically kill bees directly, they likely impair some bees' ability to forage for nectar, learn and remember where flowers are located, and find their way home to the nest or hive.

Although pesticide toxicity contributes to bee death (be it directly or indirectly), scientists agree that, in general, no single factor is responsible for the recent decline in bee populations. A collection of causes greatly contribute to the overall decline in bee populations: increasing threats from human activities, including habitat destruction and fragmentation because of urbanization; agricultural intensification; diseases and pests; and pesticide exposure. Clearly, more research needs to be done on these important threats to pollinators.

This suburban home sports beehives in the backyard. The No Spraying sign is a reminder to neighbors that any pesticides they spray on their yard also affect other yards—and any bees, seen or unseen, that live there.

Being a Good Bee Steward

While the loss of honey bee colonies and native bees may sound like small potatoes (which, by the way, do not need bees) compared to the myriad of other ills perpetrated by society and politics, it should concern everyone—at least, everyone who likes to eat. In the most extreme circumstances when pollinators are not available, humans must play the role of pollinator by literally hand-pollinating every single flower in order to assure fruit set (or eat nothing but rice, potatoes, and peanuts). This happened in 2012 in apple and pear orchards in southwest China, where wild bees have been eradicated by excessive pesticide use and a lack of habitat. People carried pots of pollen and a stick with chicken feathers into the orchards to individually hand-pollinate every flower.

Humans hand-pollinating food plants? Is this what the future holds for us? What a truly terrifying thought. But if we do not work together to combat bee deaths, habitat loss, and climate change, this could be the world we leave for our children and grandchildren. We absolutely do not want that. We tell this story not to urge you to swap out your lemonade for milk punch (or bourbon, neat) but as a stark reminder that pollinator decline is not just a local issue, no matter where your "local" is—it's a global concern, too.

You can help minimize the risk to bees and other beneficial insects by not using pesticides, insecticides or herbicides in your yard, or, if you must, by following a few simple steps:

1. Always follow the label directions on a product carefully. These directions are there to help reduce chemical exposure for nontarget organisms, including pets, bees, and people.
2. Apply neonicotinoids only to the soil, not directly to the foliage of a plant, and always apply pesticides during times when pollinators are not foraging (such as in the evening).
3. Treat only the individual plants that need treatment for a known pest infestation.

You can also help protect bees by carving out some bee-friendly space.

Urban gardens provide a refuge for pollinators trying to survive in a changing landscape.

Urban Gardens Can Make a Difference

In the past sixty years the world has undergone major landscape transformations. The majority of people around the world now live in urbanized areas, and the United States is one of the most developed countries in the world. By 2050, urbanization is expected to have increased as much as 66 percent. As urban sprawl and agricultural intensification increase, natural and peri-urban lands are replaced by buildings and impervious surfaces. Disturbed landscapes and the resulting habitat loss and fragmentation often negatively impact biodiversity; the birds and bees, along with other wildlife, are displaced as their nesting and feeding grounds disappear.

Concerns about the global decline of plant and animal species have increased interest in investigating, promoting, and conserving habitats that can support displaced flora and fauna. Luckily for those of us who are fans of enhancing biodiversity, an increasing number of folks are now very focused on protecting pollinators. Incorporating suitable habitats for pollinators throughout urban landscapes is one way to potentially offset the negative effects of urbanization on pollinators. In highly human-impacted environments, patches of undeveloped ground (such as roadsides, parks, yards, and community gardens, to name a few) become especially important for the conservation of plant and animal biodiversity. Unlike agricultural fields, these areas are generally undisturbed and therefore provide ideal nesting sites for ground-nesting bees, plant debris for cavity-nesting bees, and a variety of pollen and nectar sources to attract a wide range of insect pollinators.

Folks who support the current trend toward more community gardens and local food production in urban or peri-urban areas need to also consider pollinator habitats for those gardens to be successful. This is great news for you if you have any space at all in which to plant some flowers, and for your bees. You are getting ready to plant your very own pollinator-friendly garden.

Change Can Start in Your Backyard

Let's start with the pollinators in our backyard. Literally. Go outside and poke around. What do you see? Look not only at the plants but at the insect visitors on those plants. If you are new to insect identification, this can be an especially exciting field trip. Maybe make some notes or snap some photos. If you find that you can't immediately identify all the insects in your garden, you can spend a rainy day looking through the photos you snapped

and working to identify the beneficials (these are ones we want to keep because they are "good" and include pollinators and insects that prey on "bad" insects, which we tend to describe as pests), as well as the leaf-eating, sap-sucking pests that you do not want in your garden.

This is also a great time to start a garden journal. Write down the plants you see in your yard, what inspires you, what you like, what you would like to change, and what critters you see. You can refer to these notes as you read through this book and add to them as you are inspired by what you read or see in your garden or your community.

Get Ready to Dig In

This book will help you get started creating and maintaining your pollinator-friendly garden. In the following chapters you will learn about the major kinds of pollinators (spoiler alert: there are more than just bees!), how to select plants and design a garden to meet their needs, and how to install and maintain a pollinator-friendly garden or landscape. So get that garden journal ready and pick a comfy spot to read. We're about to explore the vast variety of pollinators in our particular, sweet tea–drinking corner of the world.

Butterflies, Bees & Beyond

When you think about insect pollinators, do you immediately think of bees? Or even maybe just the honey bee? Most of us do. How many other pollinators can you think of? Yes, butterflies are also pollinators . . . What else?

Our bet is that if you were able to name other pollinators, you had to really think about it. That's okay; we used to have trouble naming others too. The good news is that honey bees are indeed great pollinators. But there are a vast array of amazing and beautiful pollinators in the world, and we'll talk about them in this chapter. And if you're a honey bee lover, don't worry: we'll talk about them, too.

Non-Bee Pollinators

Maybe you have heard these facts and figures: pollinators are responsible for one in every three bites of food; nearly 75 percent of the world's crops require pollination; global crop production volume is estimated at as much as $577 billion a year, and in the United States honey bees contribute nearly $20 billion to the value of domestic crop production; some crops, such as almonds, are almost exclusively pollinated by managed honey bees; many crops rely on honey bees for more than 90 percent of their pollination.

While these numbers can make your head spin, they are not entirely accurate. It is true that about 35 percent of America's crops—roughly a third—rely *to some extent* on bees for pollination. Sometimes the ecosystem benefit bees bring to a crop is essential, as in the case of blueberries and cherries, which are 90 percent dependent on honey bee pollination. And yes, almonds do depend almost entirely on honey bees for pollination.

In other cases, while bees are good to have around, their absence does not result in a crisis, partly because other pollinators are present or the crop does not rely on pollination by an insect for fruit set. This in no way should dampen your enthusiasm for protecting bees! But don't forget about bugs and butterflies. We are all in this together, and we must help each other. Insect pollinators help us, so let's also help them.

It is easy to find information and facts about the importance of managed bees. However, we would like to briefly discuss the unsung heroes of the insect pollinator world—flies, butterflies, and beetles—because it is important to know what role they play in pollination when you're deciding what to plant in your pollinator habitat.

Flies: Order Diptera

In general, bees are indeed the best critter for the pollination job; with nearly 20,000 different species, bees are the most efficient pollinators. They are found all over the globe, and (they rely solely on flowers for their own food, so they are mandated to visit flowers day in and day out. But at the same time, bees are not *always* the best pollinator for the job; while not sexy, the order Diptera—mostly flies—is the second most efficient order of pollinators and is among the most diverse insect orders, with approximately 150,000 described species. Flies are less efficient at carrying pollen than bees because most of them are not as hairy as bees, but many are good pollinators nonetheless. Flies also work under much cooler conditions than bees, so they are of critical importance to wildflowers, landscape plants, and crops in cooler alpine climates.

You may be thinking, "Flies? Yuck. Just yuck." You are not alone. Many people think of flies as pests, and certainly there are many pest species. Most of us have the most experience with pest flies, including biting blackflies, common houseflies, and bluebottle flies (whose scientific name is *Calliphora vomitoria*, which pretty much says it all). Flies are also carriers of diseases. For example, houseflies can carry typhoid and salmonella, tularemia is transmitted by deerflies, and African sleeping sickness is transmitted by tsetse flies. And if that's not enough to put you off flies, then there are mosquitoes, which are also in the Diptera order. Enough said. We agree, most flies are just yuck.

Yet flies perform some beneficial activities (stick

Flies come in a wide variety of shapes, sizes, and colors. Flies are also hairy (though less hairy than bees), which makes them good pollinators, but they visit flowers primarily to drink the sugary nectar—pollination is simply a beneficial side effect. Flowers shown clockwise from above: fleabane, purple coneflower, and hydrangea.

with us here). They help control other pests; are food for valued species such as birds and fish, act as decomposers, soil conditioners, and water quality indicators (if they are in your stream, your water is healthy; if most of the insect life is gone, the stream water quality is poor and the health of the system is considered poor as well); and pollinate many plants. We consider some flies to be very important pollinators, in fact, and in a moment, they will be important to you as well, for two special little flies, the cecidomyiid and ceratopogonid midges, are essential for cocoa flower pollination. From the cocoa flower, chocolate is eventually born. (See, we told you they'd be important to you.)

Of the 150 families in the Diptera order, at least 71 include flies that feed on flowers, and more than 550 species of flowering plants are regularly visited by members of Diptera. We generally consider these flies to be pollinators, since they are moving pollen from one plant to the next. Perhaps the most important pollinators in Diptera are the flower-feeding flies, which rely on nectar from flowers to survive and therefore spend all their time flitting from flower to flower, moving those little grains of pollen around. Although Diptera is considered the second most important order of pollinating insects, members of Diptera have been documented to be the primary pollinators for many plant species, both wild and cultivated.

There are two types of fly pollination, or "fly pollination syndromes." These are known in the scientific world as "myophily" and "sapromyophily."

Sapromyophiles normally feed on dead animals or dung. These flies are attracted to odoriferous flowers that humans generally consider stinky. Have you ever passed a decomposing skunk on the road and had to roll up your windows from the awful smell? If you were a sapromyophile, you would have stopped your car in its tracks and jumped right out to lay eggs on that carcass. If that carcass had turned out to be a skunk cabbage, you would have had dinner there as well.

Myophiles, particularly bee flies (family Bombyliidae) and hoverflies (family Syrphidae), regularly feed on nectar and pollen. Myophiles are attracted to plants that do not have a strong scent and that are purple, violet, blue, and/or white; single-whorled with an exposed center; or tube-shaped. Both types of myophiles look like bees to the untrained eye, and they are frequently mistaken for bees at first glance. Upon closer inspection, however, you might notice their especially long "beak" and streamlined thorax with a single pair of wings (not two pairs of wings, as would be found on the bees and wasps in the Hymenoptera order). Bee flies' close resemblance to bees earned these shaggy critters their name. In the case of hoverflies, their common name comes from their habit of literally hovering around flowers.

Hoverflies tend to prefer yellow-colored flowers but also can frequently be found on white or pink flowers. Although hoverflies are often considered mainly nonselective or generalist pollinators, some hoverflies species are highly selective and visit and carry pollen from a single plant species. Hoverflies can be important in a landscape for more than simply pollination purposes. While the adult flies are not predaceous, the larvae do prey on insect pests commonly found in home gardens. Hoverfly eggs resemble small grains of rice and are laid singly on leaves, usually in or near an aphid colony. When they hatch, the larvae (also called maggots) have

voracious appetites; a single maggot will devour hundreds of aphids during its roughly two-week development period. Hoverfly larvae also prey on thrips and scale insects, making them well worth encouraging in an ecologically friendly pollinator-friendly garden.

Interested in practicing your bee fly– and hoverfly-spotting skills? In our gardens, we most often find them on yarrow (genus *Achillea*), especially 'Moonbeam', although they also like catnip, basil, and plants (both desired and not) in the Apiaceae family, such as dill (*Anethum graveolens*), fennel (*Foeniculum vulgare*), and Queen Anne's lace (*Daucus carota*).

Some insects try very hard to imitate bees (we call them "bee mimics"), and they often do a surprisingly good job of it. These photos show a bee fly (left) and hoverfly (right). Both flies are commonly mistaken for bees.

While butterflies generally make poor pollinators, this black swallowtail butterfly is doing its part by pollinating a butterfly bush. Notice the pollen grains clinging to the small hairs on its thorax and abdomen.

Recent research suggests that in the South, flies primarily pollinate small flowers that bloom in the shade and grow in seasonally moist habitats. These plants include Dutchman's pipe (*Aristolochia macrophylla*), flowering dogwood (*Cornus florida*), dead horse arum (*Helicodiceros muscivorous*), oakleaf hydrangea (*Hydrangea quercifolia*), and skunk cabbage (*Symplocarpus foetidus*).

Butterflies and Moths: Order Lepidoptera

Welcome in any garden, lepidopterans are members of one of the most widespread and widely recognizable insect orders in the world. Butterflies and moths visit flowers for food, unfurling their long proboscis (the lepidopteran version of a tongue) to probe the flowers and lazily drink in the sugary nectar. You have probably enjoyed watching skippers or fritillaries feed on large, flamboyant flowers. They are a joy to observe as they flit from flower to flower, probing with their proboscis, drinking the sweet nectar from the base of these attractive flowers. As you might expect, in the process of foraging, a butterfly brushes against the flower's stamen, lightly dislodging the pollen, and collects the pollen on its legs, then flies to the next flower. The pollen, which is held very loosely, is then deposited on the stigma of the next flower.

However, not much pollen is transferred, for

A butterfly prefers very different foods as a larva (caterpillar) and as an adult, largely due to the differences in its mouth parts. Caterpillars use chewing mouth parts to eat leaves and flowers. Adult butterflies drink their food through a tubelike tongue called a proboscis. At left, a swallowtail caterpillar on golden Alexander; at right, a painted lady butterfly on a purple coneflower.

several reasons. Because a proboscis is long and skinny, a lepidopteran's body does not come into close contact with the flower. And unlike the thorax (body) of a bee, the thorax of a butterfly is not designed to capture pollen grains, so under most conditions lepidopterans collect little pollen. Some research suggests that pollen does sometimes collect inside a butterfly's facial cavity, and when the proboscis unfurls at the next feeding, this pollen can be transferred in small amounts to the flower. Pollen grains can also occasionally be found on the thorax and legs, but research has shown that this pollen is not transferred to subsequent flowers in appreciable amounts. But while butterflies

contribute little to the overall pollination needs of plants, they cannot be discounted completely. Since many lepidopterans travel long distances in a single day, butterflies and moths play an important role as long-distance carriers of pollen and can aid in increased gene flow, resulting in greater genetic variation in some plant populations.

Although butterflies make poor pollinators, it is worth mentioning that a few plants rely almost exclusively on butterflies for pollination. The herbaceous perennial maiden pink (*Dianthus deltoides*) is commonly used for ground cover in gardens with well-drained soil and lots of sun. These sweet little plants are psychophilious—adapted especially for butterfly pollination—and are visited by butterflies for nectar and flies for pollen. Research conducted on maiden pink demonstrated that seed set was greater for flowers frequently visited by butterflies. This underscores that while most scientists regard butterflies as unimportant and poor pollinators in quantitative terms, they are of great importance if you are a maiden pink or another plant that relies on them.

When selecting plants to encourage butterflies to visit your garden or landscape, choose ones that have the form and colors that butterflies prefer. The most attractive plants are good nectar producers, such as butterfly bush (*Buddleia* sp.), which, yes, is not native to the South and is even considered invasive in some states, but is still an excellent food source for anthophilous (flower-feeding) insects of all kinds. (In fact, Danesha has seen as many as seven different pollinator species on a single bush at the same time!) Other good nectar producers include asters (*Symphyotrichum* spp.), goldenrods (*Solidago* spp.), mint (*Mentha* spp.), spotted Joe-pye weed (*Eutrochium maculatum*), coneflowers (*Echinacea* spp.), bee balm (*Monarda fistulosa*), Mexican sunflowers (*Tithonia rotundifolia*), and milkweed (*Asclepias* spp.), just to name a few.

In order to maximize foraging efficiency, lepidopterans, like most animals, are attracted to the plants that are most favorable to them. Butterflies' taste receptors are located chiefly on the palpi, small sensory projections that protrude from the head, and on the tarsi, the feet; yes, they taste what they walk on! They are drawn to flowers' smell, color, and form. Butterflies are most attracted to bright colors, including blue, yellow, orange, and especially red. They also prefer zygomorphic (bilaterally symmetrical)

and tubelike flowers, such as columbine (*Aquilegia canadensis*), beardtongue (*Penstemon digitalis*), and snapdragon (*Antirrhinum majus*). Because butterflies are most active in full sun, most of their favorite flowers are ideal for sunny garden spots.

To draw butterflies to your garden, it is also important to include food sources for caterpillars; the butterflies will lay their eggs on these host plants, and when the larvae hatch, they will feed on them, chewing through the delicious leaves and depositing frass (pelletized caterpillar poop) in their wake. Some lepidopterans, such as monarch butterflies and pipevine swallowtails, deposit their eggs on only one kind of plant, but not all lepidopterans are so discriminating. A few common host plants for familiar butterflies include plants in the pea (Fabaceae) and mallow (Malvaceae) families for the gray hairstreak, and purple coneflowers (*Echinacea purpurea*) and sunflowers (*Helianthus annuus*) for painted lady butterflies. Gulf fritillaries love passionflower vines (*Passiflora incarnata*), and the snakelike spicebush swallowtail caterpillars hide in the folded leaves of the spicebush plant (*Lindera benzoin*) during the day and come out to feed on those same leaves in the evenings.

Black swallowtail larvae are commonly referred to as "parsley caterpillars" because that is one of their most common host plants. Black swallowtails also lay eggs on dill, fennel, and Queen Anne's lace; when the eggs hatch, the larvae will readily defoliate these plants. This is something to keep in mind when planting host plants for caterpillars: the caterpillars will eat these leaves with a hearty appetite, leaving little but leaf veins and frass behind.

Milkweeds are important for monarch butterflies, which lay their eggs exclusively on their leaves

Some species of butterflies rely on specific plants or plant families as hosts for their eggs and food for the caterpillars. These caterpillars are the larval stages of the spicebush swallowtail on a spicebush (A), black swallowtail on dill (B), and variegated fritillary on a passionflower (C).

and stems of milkweed plants. When the eggs hatch, the caterpillars feed on the plant's toxic sap. For most other insects this latex-based sap is poisonous, but monarch caterpillars not only are able to feed on it safely but become toxic themselves by doing so. This ultimately helps to protect the caterpillars and adult butterflies from predation by birds and other animals that would otherwise try to make them dinner.

Although milkweed is the monarch butterfly's only host plant, there are many different species of milkweed that monarchs can use, though some species seem to be preferred. Some of our favorite *Asclepias* species for gardens in the South include swamp milkweed (*Asclepias incarnata*), butterfly weed (*Asclepias tuberosa*), and the hard-to-find but beautiful purple milkweed (*Asclepias purpurascens*). A favorite overwintering plant for monarchs in Florida is tropical milkweed (*Asclepias curassavica*). It is common to see monarch butterflies feeding on tropical milkweed nectar while their fat, green, hungry caterpillar babies feed on the plant's leaves.

A lesser-known pollinator-plant relationship is between the pipevine swallowtail butterfly and its primary host plant, Dutchman's pipe. Like milkweed, Dutchman's pipe contains chemicals that are distasteful and toxic to most insects that ingest it. Pipevine swallowtail caterpillars are able to process and accumulate these chemicals without harm to themselves, and like monarchs, they, too, become toxic to their potential predators. This chemical protection extends through metamorphosis to the adult butterfly, thus protecting the mature butterfly from predation.

Monarchs and other butterfly species take advantage of Florida's warm climate and the prevalence of native and nonnative tropical milkweed year-round.

Not All Milkweeds Are Good for Butterflies

Tropical milkweed is a readily available milkweed that's not native to the United States. It was planted by many swept up in the "save the monarch" craze. This trend is still popular today thanks in part to efforts by the federal government (specifically, the U.S. Fish and Wildlife Service) and nonprofit educational outreach programs such as Monarch Watch and the Monarch Joint Venture. Unlike native milkweeds, it does not die back in the winter in warmer states, such as Texas and Florida. Monarch butterflies are attracted to this plant, and instead of heading to Mexico for the winter, as they are supposed to, monarchs that feast on these tropical milkweeds choose the lazy approach and remain on these milkweeds through the winter.

The problem is that tropical milkweed can be host to a protozoan parasite called *Ophryocystis elektroscirrha*. Monarch caterpillars ingest the parasite along with their normal milkweed forage, and when they hatch from their chrysalides, they are covered in spores. These parasite-laden butterflies are weak and less likely to survive to migrate as adults.

Beetles: Order Coleoptera

Beetles and wasps are also anthophilous insects that are thought of as pollinators, but scientists know next to nothing about their pollinator habits and capabilities.

Let's start with beetles. You know beetles; they crunch when you step on them (whether on purpose or by accident), and we either love them (ladybugs, which should actually be called lady beetles, as they are not actually bugs but beetles) or hate them (Japanese beetles). They have a particularly hard exoskeleton and forewings that are not used for flying. They also have antennae, which are their primary sensory organs and can detect motion, odor, and chemical substances—like cat whiskers, they detect their physical environment.

When talking about whether theology has anything to learn from science, the British biologist J. B. S. Haldane famously said that God must have "an inordinate fondness for beetles." And in fact, it does seem to be so. Around 380,000 species of beetles have already been described and recognized, and it's commonly believed that there are many more that have yet to be described and classified. Beetles account for a quarter of all known animal species. There are more species of lady beetles alone than of mammals, of longhorn beetles than of birds, of weevils than of fish.

Beetles can exploit a wide range of food sources that are as varied as their habitats. Some beetles are omnivores, eating both plants and animals. Others are highly specialized in their diet. Beetles were the first pollinators, and it is thought that they are responsible for pollinating some 88 percent of the 240,000 flowering plants around the world. Because beetles eat pollen, they prefer

Beetles are incredibly diverse. There are a great number of beetles that pollinate flowers such as portulaca and yarrow.

their flowers to be shaped like bowls (like magnolia flowers), to have many tiny clustered flowers (like goldenrods), and/or to have exposed anthers and shed pollen easily (like rattlesnake master, *Eryngium yuccifolium*). Beetle-pollinated flowers also tend to be large, greenish or off-white in color, and heavily scented. Beetles prefer scents that are spicy, fruity, or like decaying organic material. Essentially, beetles do not like to work too hard for their food, so they tend to be attracted to plants that offer easy access to pollen. As they travel from flower to flower eating pollen, they drop bits of pollen on the next flower they visit.

A wasp's thin waistline is one of its most noticeable physical features and easily distinguishes it from most bees. Shown here are two different wasps, one on a pink coreopsis and the other on a hyssop.

Wasps: Order Hymenoptera

Wasps are in the same order as bees and ants: Hymenoptera. Like beetles, wasps are not covered with fuzzy hairs, making pollen less likely to stick to their smooth bodies and less easily transported from flower to flower. So, like beetles, wasps make inefficient pollinators. However, for some plant species, wasps are an incredibly important mutualist pollinator. A favorite example is the fig (*Ficus carica*), a common tree in yards across the South. Figs, an unusual and tasty fruit, are unique in that their flowers are actually inside the immature fruit. A tiny critter called a fig wasp (superfamily Chalci-doidea) is responsible for pollinating our southern figs, as well as the almost 1,000 species of figs in the tropics. The fig wasps enter the fruit through a tiny pore to mate and lay eggs, and in the process, they pollinate the tiny flowers inside the fig fruit. Oh, and then the female fig wasps die. Right there. In the fruit. However, the crunchy bits you eat when you bite into a fig are indeed the seeds and not wasp carcasses. An enzyme in the fig called ficin breaks down the little wasp carcasses into protein, and then the fig basically digests the dead insect, using it to nourish the ripened fruit. (And now you can eat figs again. You're welcome.)

Herbs are among the most pollinator-friendly plants. Lavender and anything in the mint family, such as oregano and catmint, are especially attractive to bees.

Wasps may be poor pollinators, but there are other reasons to learn to appreciate wasps. Some wasps are considered beneficial not for their pollination habits but for their penchant for killing and eating other insects. These wasps do not sting, because their stingers have evolved to allow the females to lay eggs in the bodies of other insects. The eggs then hatch, and the young feed on the host insect from the inside, eventually killing it. After the larvae have killed the pest (because most of the host insects are insects we gardeners consider pests), only hollow "mummies" are left behind, and it is goodbye, nasty pest.

Two of these beneficial wasps in the family Ampulicidae (cockroach wasps) are found in the South. *Ampulex canaliculata* is widespread in the eastern part of the United States, from Massachu-

setts to Georgia and Arkansas, and *Ampulex ferruginea* is exclusively found in the South, from Texas to Florida. These little ladies sting cockroaches twice in order to inject venom into the host's brain. What happens next is so strange, it almost sounds as though it's direct from a science fiction novel: the venom leaves the cockroach with the ability to walk, but it is entirely robbed of the power to initiate its own movement. In an article in *National Geographic*, Ed Yong writes that "in this befuddled state, the . . . wasp can grab the roach by its antennae and walk it around like a dog on a leash." The wasp leads her pet cockroach to her nest, where she lays an egg in its belly. The egg eventually hatches. The larvae then use the still-alive-but-unable-to-move cockroach as food.

The good news is that these (eventually very

dead) insects that are terrorized by wasps are generally considered pests in gardens and on farms. This means that serial killers of these pest insects are placed in a category we call "beneficial insects." Many smaller wasp species fall into this category, and while they're not pollinators, they are a nice addition to any home garden.

A great many of the plants that are valuable for bees and butterflies are also great at attracting parasitic wasps. If you are especially interested in plants that attract beneficial wasps, you might consider including common yarrow (*Achillea millefolium*), sea lavender (*Limonium latifolium*), and rattlesnake master in your gardens.

Herbs are always a nice addition to any garden for the obvious culinary reasons, but with the additional benefit of attracting parasitic wasps and many types of pollinators. Some of our favorites include dill and fennel (both are also especially great for hosting swallowtail larvae), oregano (*Origanum vulgare*), rosemary (*Salvia rosmarinus*), basil (*Ocimum basilicum*), or lavender (*Lavandula augustifolia*). Marigolds (*Tagetes erecta*) are another great companion plant that attract parasitic wasps and deter garden pests.

Bees: Order Hymenoptera— Saving the Best for Last

Let's see, we've covered flies, butterflies, beetles, wasps . . . Ah, we have reached bees! Bees truly are important to our agricultural systems, our ecological systems, and our gardens. Furthermore, in 2015 it was estimated that bees contribute around $14 million to the U.S. agriculture economy via pollination. They are also, very often, the very best polli-nators. They are fuzzy, frenetic, and have a built-in sense of duty and family (the social bees do, anyway). Bees, in short, are great.

Even though we know that bees are very important to agricultural production and both wild and planted landscapes, scientists really know very little about them. For example, how do honey bees fit into the greater community of pollinators and our ecosystems, despite the fact that they are not native to the United States? How will climate change affect bee pollinators, flowering plants, and their interactions? Do bee hotels increase bee populations or act as means of disease transmission? The list of what we don't know could go on and on. From a strictly ecological standpoint, what we do know is that that globally there are over 20,000 bee species, with just over 4,000 species in North America, and new species are being found (and lost) every year. In general, bees range in size from less than two millimeters to about one and a half inches and come in a multitude of colors, including metallic green, reddish-brown, and black with yellow and orange stripes.

To best understand how to design and plant a garden to attract these magnificent creatures and to promote insect conservation, it is best to understand bees from a basic level. What makes a bee a bee? How can we use what we know about their behavior and life cycle, to build a better pollinator garden? This section will introduce these fundamentals.

An Introduction to Social Bees

Bees, like humans, can be social or solitary. Some social species, including honey bees, bumblebees, and stingless bees, live together in large colonies.

Killer Bees

Although the term "killer bee" is primarily used in popular press stories and in the movies, not by scientists, there's no denying that these bees are extremely aggressive. So-called killer bees are a human-assisted hybrid of European and African honey bees that escaped into the wild. After beginning their reign of terror in Brazil in 1957, these bees rapidly spread through South and Central America. They made their way to Arizona sometime in the early 1990s and other southern states thereafter. Africanized honey bees have been found consistently in Florida, Texas, Oklahoma, and Louisiana. There are also reports that these bees have been seen but are not necessarily established (meaning they are not found year-round and, so far, have only been spotted passing through) in Arkansas, Alabama, Georgia, and South Carolina.

It cannot be overstated how vicious these bees can be. Africanized honey bees will attack people and animals who inadvertently stray into their territory, seriously injuring or even killing them. We have heard firsthand reports coming out of Arizona of Africanized honey bees chasing down golfers who unwittingly tried to find their Titleist Pro V1 ball in an "out of play" and bee-inhabited area on a golf course. In the recent account we heard, this golfer lived, although he had to abandon his search in order to run screaming into the irrigation pond, but not all reports of people coming into contact with these bees end with the loss of only a golf ball.

It is nearly impossible to tell an Africanized honey bee from a common honey bee, so if you live in one of the states that has Africanized honey bees, it is best to call in an expert before trying to wrangle an errant swarm. Which is actually good advice with any bee swarm: do not engage it and call an expert.

These colonies are established by swarms consisting of a queen and several hundred workers. Honey bees frequently develop a perennial nest that remains year after year, making them excellent "management material." Social bees have the ability to regulate the colony's temperature and thus can survive in extremely hot or cold environments. They are highly evolved insects that engage in a variety of complex tasks not practiced by the multitude of solitary bees. Communication, nest construction, environmental control, hive protection, and division of the labor are just some of the behaviors that social bees have developed to exist successfully in social colonies. The family Apidae contains three distinct groups that exhibit eusocial behavior: bumblebees, honey bees, and a group

Africanized bees (left) are slightly smaller than the gentle, better-known European honey bee (right), but otherwise they're nearly identical. When in doubt, it is best not to stick around to compare sizes! Both are shown enjoying blanketflowers.

known as stingless bees, about which scientists know very little, so I am only going to discuss the more common social bees.

HONEY BEES

Honey bees, arguably the most well-known social bees, are an Old World species thought to have originated in Asia. They are in the genus *Apis*, which is thought to be named after the Egyptian word for "sacred bull." There are currently seven species of *Apis* bees recognized worldwide. Asian *Apis* bees gave rise to both the eastern honey bee (*Apis cerana*) and the western honey bee (*Apis mellifera*), the only bee species that now has worldwide distribution. There are twenty-nine subspecies of *A. mellifera*, but we tend to refer to all of them as simply "honey bees." These are native to Europe, the Middle East, and Africa (notice we did *not* say North America).

A. mellifera is a highly social insect that lives in relatively large colonies consisting of three morphologically distinct types—queen, drone, and worker—with a complex division of labor. The western honey bee is best known for its production of honey, a sweet that humans have craved for centuries; when *Homo sapiens* migrated from the Old World to the New in the seventeenth century, they took along honey bees to help feed their sweet tooth, and like the ancestors of those original colonists, honey bees are also now found in all fifty states.

Although an extreme example of bad bee encounters, the Africanized honey bee may be the only bee we need to be seriously concerned with—unless you have a real bee venom allergy, there's little need to be afraid of most bees. Social bees have been known to sting, of course, but they do so only when provoked or under terrible stress. You can greatly reduce your chances of getting stung by simply being aware of your surroundings. (Walking barefoot through a bee-friendly lawn full of blooming white clover? Do not be surprised if you get stung!) Bees primarily sting when they feel they must protect their hive, so if you are near a bee colony, whether it's a hive in a tree or a human-built box, stay a respectful distance away and resist swatting at the bees (this is typically called "the commonsense approach"). With bees, as with angry toddlers, swatting and yelling does not encourage them to settle down. Furthermore, threatened bees are attracted to movement, and while it has not been proven scientifically, it is probably a good bet that hitting them just upsets them more. Don't want to be stung? Don't swat at bees.

Honey bees may be best known for their lives in hives. When these bees are not nesting in a manufactured hive, they usually nest above ground, often inside hollow trees. Wherever their hives are located, they construct vertical wax combs with individual hexagonal cells for storing honey and rearing their young. Each hive has a single queen whose only job is to lay eggs. The hive also contains tens of thousands of female workers and, during the spring and summer months, anywhere from several hundred to several thousand male drones. The worker bees perform all labor necessary to keep the hive alive, including collecting nectar and pollen, producing wax and honey, feeding the young, and protecting the hive against enemies. Adult workers live for only about six weeks, while queens may last for several years.

A drone is the product of an unfertilized egg laid by either the queen or a worker bee. Drones have bigger eyes than workers and lack stingers. They cannot help defend the hive and do not have the body parts necessary for collecting pollen or nectar, so they do not contribute to any sort of housekeeping within the hive. Drones are generally described as serving a single purpose: to find a new queen and mate with her. Or, as one paper written in 1912 put it, "Honeybee drones are often called 'lazy Willi' and are often assumed to merely function as 'flying sperm,' necessary to inseminate virgin queens." This may be a bit harsh, and as it turns out, it's not completely accurate. Recent research suggests that older drones also help reduce heat buildup in a hive under extreme thermal stress conditions.

No matter the potential contribution, a drone's job is a fatal one. When a drone mates with a queen and releases his semen, it happens with such force that his endophallus is ripped from his abdomen. Unsurprisingly, he usually dies shortly thereafter. If a drone is not one of the ten to fifteen drones that mate with the queen during her mating flight, he must head back to the hive to lay about. In the fall, when food becomes scarce, he becomes just another (useless) mouth to feed. Therefore, worker bees starve the drones to weaken them, then escort them to the hive entrance and literally toss them out of the hive. The drones eventually die from hypothermia or starvation.

BUMBLEBEES

Bumblebees are important pollinators of agricultural and wild plants and are the primary pollinators of greenhouse-grown crops such as tomatoes, peppers, and eggplants. While these plants are self-fertile, they benefit from bumblebee visits because bumblebees' special sonicating wings help release pollen from the flower. Unlike other bees that passively collect pollen on hairs, bumblebees collect pollen from some plants by grasping flowers and vibrating their flight muscles, ergo sonication. In addition, many berry crops—including blueberries, cranberries, and caneberries—benefit from bumblebee pollination, as do other fruits, including apricots, apples, melons, and squashes, and seed crops, such as alfalfa, clover, and onions. Bumblebees also provide a pop of color and sound to a garden, and watching these busy ladies forage in your garden can bring a sense of joy. It's relatively easy to tell bumblebees apart with a little training. Bumblebees can frequently be found clinging to flowers after a rainstorm, making this a good time to practice your bumblebee-identifying skills.

Of the forty-five species of bumblebees in the United States, only about four are especially feisty. Because bumblebees are eusocial, they can be raised in managed hives just like honey bees (only smellier), and many of the non-feisty species have indeed been raised by scientists in laboratories or by bumblebee keepers. Wild bumblebees, however, tend to nest in the ground in cavities such as abandoned rodent burrows, holes in building foundations, or stacks of wood.

The life cycle of the bumblebee begins in spring, when rising temperatures awaken a lone hibernating queen bumblebee. The queen has spent the entire winter underground, using up reserves of energy stored as fat in her body. When she first emerges, she seeks out nectar-rich flowers in order to gain energy through the sugar in the nectar. Her next step is to find a new home. Once the queen finds a suitable site, she begins preparing the nest space by building a small wax cup, called a honey pot, and collecting pollen, which she will use to feed her developing brood. Once the nest is provisioned, she lays eggs on the pollen lump and begins incubating the eggs by laying her abdomen over them to keep them warm. After this point, the queen remains in the nest unless she needs to collect more food. Depending on the weather, the first workers begin to hatch anywhere from twenty-one to twenty-eight days after the eggs were laid. When the eggs hatch, the female workers, already adults, immediately begin taking care of foraging, cleaning the nest, and caring for the brood.

Worker honey bees' job depends on their age, a

Male bumblebees and carpenter bees are easily identified by the yellow "mustache" on their face. Here on a salvia, the male carpenter bee on the upper right is easily distinguished from the female carpenter bee on the lower left.

phenomenon bee beekeepers call "age-related division of labor." When workers are just a day or two old, their job to clean the cells, starting with the one they were born in. They also keep the brood warm. A few days later, they begin to feed older larvae. By the time they are six to eleven days old, they are responsible enough to feed the youngest larvae. By the ripe old age of twelve to seventeen days, they are producing wax, carrying food, building combs, and carrying out undertaker duties. At twenty days

old they protect the hive entrance and have guard duty. In their final days, from about twenty-two to forty or forty-five days old, the worker bees take foraging trips to gather pollen, nectar, water, and other needed resources. Interestingly, not all workers do all the jobs, and depending on what the hive needs at the time, workers might skip some tasks as they mature.

As the spring progresses, nests begin producing offspring that are not workers. The new queens and males will allow the colony to reproduce. The male bees leave the nest and do not return. They do not collect pollen and spend their time feeding on nectar and trying to mate. The new queens leave the nest and mate soon after. Mating behavior varies between species but typically involves several males competing in one way or another. After mating, the males die, and the queens feed briefly before digging a hibernacula (a protective case made of leaves or other materials in which an animal hides or hibernates) and becoming dormant for the winter.

While bumblebee and honey bee colonies are similar in some ways, there are also some differences in how they're organized. Bumblebee colonies are annual; just as annual flowers die completely each year, with only the seeds surviving, so too do bumblebee colonies start from scratch every year. Also, their colonies are generally much smaller than those of honey bees, although the number of bees per colony varies widely among species and can range anywhere from fewer than 100 to more than 400 females. Although bumblebees also have a division of labor, with some worker bees specializing in foraging or nest work, a bumblebee's age is not nearly as good a predictor of her job as a honey

Clockwise from top left: Hyssop, coneflowers, and milkweed are all excellent bee-friendly plants. But the easiest plant to grow that's beloved by bees of all types is clover.

bee's age is. For bumblebees, size is a better predictor: larger workers tend to spend more time foraging, and smaller workers work more in the nest.

Unlike honey bees, queen and worker bumblebees look basically the same, although queens are typically larger. In some species, worker bumblebees fight with each other and the queen and try to lay eggs. The queen maintains her status as the prime egg layer of the colony by attacking other bees aggressively, eating worker eggs, and producing signaling chemicals (pheromones, which elicit a behavioral or physiological response by another animal of the same species). At the end of autumn, the queen, males, and most of the workers of the colony die, leaving a few large, healthy females destined to become queens to overwinter. These females will set off on their own to start new colonies the following spring.

Common Bumblebees in the South

Two-spotted bumblebee: Its range extends all the way from Maine to Florida and from the coast west to Illinois, Kansas, Oklahoma, and Tennessee, but it does not include Alabama, Mississippi, Louisiana, or Arkansas. Queens emerge in April, workers are active from May through August, and the males are seen from June through October. Their preferred flowers include roses, goldenrods, and St. John's wort.

Southern Plains bumblebee: Its range extends from New Jersey to Florida and from the coast west to North Dakota, South Dakota, Nebraska, Colorado, and New Mexico.

Brown-belted bumblebee: Its range is quite broad, including most of the United States and even parts of Quebec.

Common eastern bumblebee: They are truly common, found from Ontario and Maine to Florida and as far west as Louisiana and Arkansas. Queens typically emerge in April, and queens, workers, and males are active through October in the South. Their preferred flowers include goldenrods and thistles.

American bumblebee: Its range extends from Ontario to Maryland and south to Florida, then west to Minnesota, South Dakota, Nebraska, Colorado, New Mexico, and Mexico.

Yellow-banded bumblebee: Originally, this species extended from Nova Scotia to Florida and west to British Columbia, Montana, and South Dakota. While once common, it has declined dramatically since 1990. Now it is mainly found in small pockets in eastern part of the United States.

An Introduction to Solitary Bees

Although honey bees are legendary for their complex cooperative lifestyle, the vast majority of bee species are solitary. In fact, solitary bees make up approximately 90 percent of the bee species in the United States. These bees are not only less aggressive but also less well-known, and certainly less well-studied. Despite the lack of scientific research on solitary bees, these little critters are very important. From a conservation and agricultural standpoint, and for the purposes of this book, it is not necessary to recognize all the different bee species. It is important, however, to know that there is great biodiversity among bee species, especially among solitary bees. And these solitary creatures are incredibly important for healthy ecosystems, including cropping systems and gardens alike, so both diversity and abundance in bee fauna is important.

With around 4,000 species in the United States,

Native bees come in all shapes, colors, and sizes. While some are easy to spot, like the common eastern bumblebee (top left), others are almost too small to see, like the sweat bee on this bright yellow St. John's wort flower (top right). Other interesting bees include the shiny green sweat bee (bottom right) on native blanketflower and the distinctive leafcutter bee (bottom left) on a prickly pear.

from the tiny sweat bee to the large carpenter bee, bees are found anywhere flowers bloom. In the American South, 500 native bee species have been reported in North Carolina and Georgia and roughly 200 in Louisiana, and a new scientific paper that came out in 2018 describes 191 native bee species in Mississippi. As you can see, there is a great deal of variety in the South, and not just in our taste in barbecue sauce!

In the South, native bees come in a wide range of sizes and shapes, build a variety of kinds of nests, visit a variety of flowers, and are active in a variety of seasons. Here we will focus on the bees most prevalent across the South, those you are

The furrow bee (left) is one of the most abundant and readily identifiable bees in North Carolina. It's characterized by its penchant for mining or burrowing into the ground to create a nest (shown at right). Furrow bees are a generalist species and will pollinate a variety of different plants in the course of a single foraging trip.

most likely to come across in your backyard and the ones most likely to be impacted by your garden and management strategies.

FURROW BEES AND SWEAT BEES

Bees in the family Halictidae, which includes furrow bees and sweat bees, are easy to identify by their metallic appearance, although some are shinier than others. The over 200 species in the genus *Halictus*, which are found primarily in the Northern Hemisphere, exhibit different social behaviors depending on climate: they're solitary in cooler regions but eusocial in warmer ones, and in some areas of the South, they tend to be either communal or semisocial. They are active from about March through November. A few species in the genus have

extensive geographic distribution, such as *Halictus rubicundus* and *H. confusus*. Most halictids create in-ground nests, or burrows, in sand or loose soil, in areas with little to no vegetation or other cover, such as mulch. Both solitary and eusocial halictids tend to build their burrows on south-facing slopes, which allows for a toasty-warm nest, thanks to the passive solar heating of the surrounding soil.

Halictids are the classic generalist foragers. To paraphrase the early-twentieth-century humorist Will Rogers, they have never met a flower they did not like. They gather pollen and nectar from many different plant species, even in a single foraging trip. Despite their generalist foraging behavior, sweat bees are very important pollinators for many wildflowers and crops, including stone fruits,

Sweat bees are widespread and abundant throughout North America. These brightly colored, metallic-green or blue bees are generalist foragers with short tongues and prefer to forage on flowers that have shallow, easily accessible nectar, such as liatris.

MINING BEES

The family Andrenidae has the most species of any bee family, and new species are discovered almost every year. Bees in this family are typically small, digging bees roughly the same size as or smaller than honey bees. Unlike honey bees, mining bees live a solitary lifestyle, and as their name implies, they build nests in burrows in the ground, often in aggregations, usually in sparsely vegetated areas. Mining bees are active primarily in the spring. Their presence often alarms homeowners because of the holes they dig in bare patches of lawn and because a large number of males swarm in these areas. There is no need for concern if you see this. Most of the bees that are buzzing around are males, and they lack the ability to sting. And don't worry, they are not killing your grass; they are simply taking advantage of bare areas where grass is already thin. Mining bees only swarm for a few weeks in the spring. Even if this is unnerving, do not reach for a can of wasp spray! You can, however, water the area, which generally encourages them to move elsewhere to nest.

pome fruits, alfalfa, and sunflowers. Populations of these bees can be encouraged by planting suitable wildflower and providing nesting areas (reduce the use of mulch wherever possible and keep tillage or cultivation to a minimum). Essentially, if you plant flowers that produce pollen and/or nectar, you are going to get these busy little bees.

It is easy to spot the metallic green sweat bee, from the genus *Agapostemon*, from April through October. These generalist foragers are common on golden Alexanders (*Zizia aurea*), coneflowers, and asters.

LEAFCUTTER BEES

Bees in the family Megachilidae are important native pollinators in the American South, where the number of reported species ranges from eight in Kentucky to thirty-five in North Carolina; these species include *Megachile pruina* and *Megachile rubi*. There are more *Megachile* species in the American West, but the distribution of many species is not well known because of the lack of data. Furthermore, many leafcutter bees are missing in action. A large proportion of species (19 percent) are known only from historical records and have

Leafcutter bees cut crescent-shaped sections out of leaves and flowers to use as nesting material, leaving the plant with leaves like these. These gentle bees are active in the warm summer months and are perfect for pollinating squash, melons, cucumbers, peas, and other summer vegetables and fruits.

not been reported for at least twenty-five years, usually much longer.

Most leafcutter bees are around the size of a honey bee, between five millimeters and twenty-four millimeters long, with stout black bodies. They get their name from their habit of cutting leaves to use for constructing nests in cavities (mostly in rotting wood or hollow grasses). They create multiple cells in the nest, each with a single egg and pollen for the larva to eat after it hatches.

Leafcutter bees use the leaves of almost any broad-leaved deciduous plant to construct their nests. Some species of leafcutter bees use petals and resin in addition to leaves. Females perch on a leaf and cut in a circle or half-moon around themselves. When the leaf fragment is severed from the rest of the leaf, the female flies to her nest clutching the piece of leaf. Ornamental plants with thin, smooth leaves, such as roses (*Rosa* spp.), azaleas (*Rhododendron* spp.), redbuds (*Cercis canadensis*), and bougainvilleas (*Bougainvillea glabra*), are preferred. Although the cutting can destroy a plant's aesthetics, it rarely harms the plant. Placing physical barriers such as cheesecloth on susceptible plants as soon as the cut leaves are seen can prevent further damage.

Female leafcutter bees are incredibly efficient pollinators, purportedly doing the work of twenty honey bees in one foraging trip. These ladies carry pollen on hairs on the underside of their abdomen, rather than on their hind legs like other bees. These bees are easily identified when laden with pollen because the underside of the abdomen often appears light yellow to deep gold in color.

Leafcutter bees are important pollinators of wildflowers, fruits, vegetables, and other crops.

Bee hotels like the three shown here are as varied as the bees that use them. They are also easy to build with your kids as a weekend project and can be placed anywhere you think bees would be welcomed.

Mason bees (*Osmia* spp.), a genus in the leafcutter family, are used by commercial growers to pollinate blueberries and alfalfa.

Leafcutter bees do not aggressively defend nesting areas like the more social honey bees and bumblebees. Their sting has been described as far less painful than that of a honey bee (we have been fortunate enough to never have been stung by a leafcutter bee). Leafcutter bees are typically described as docile and will sting only if handled.

If you would like to encourage leafcutter bees to visit your garden (don't laugh! They are pollinators, they add to the biodiversity of your landscape, and you can think of the precisely cut leaves as gar-

den art!), you can create nesting areas for them by bundling hollow reeds or bamboo stems (cut at a joint so the reed or stem is closed on one end), or by drilling holes in a block of wood.

CUCKOO BEES

Cuckoo bees are a group of related species that are descended from "true" bumblebees and fall in the family Apidae (along with honey bees and bumblebees). Cuckoo bees, similar to their namesake, the cuckoo bird, use the nests of true bumblebees to raise their own offspring.

The female cuckoo bee enters the nest of the unsuspecting bumblebee and often hides in the nest debris for a while. Eventually the cuckoo female kills the bumblebee queen and lays her own eggs in a provisioned brood cell. The worker bumblebees then unwittingly raise the offspring of the cuckoo bee. The cuckoo bee larvae become adult bees, leave the nest, and mate with other cuckoo bees, and then the females go into hibernation and begin the cycle again.

These bees are frequently observed on flowers in late spring and early fall. Common forage plants for cuckoo bees include goat's beard (*Aruncus dioicus*), yarrow, goldenrods, and asters.

Pollinators Are Worth Protecting

E. O. Wilson once said of ants, "We need them to survive, but they don't need us at all."

Think about that. It is true of not just ants but also flies, beetles, bees, and even mosquitoes. Species live together everywhere on our hot, crowded planet, and we all depend on one another (some more than others, of course). A biodiverse planet, with a great number of species of plants, animals, insects, microorganisms, and fungi, is a richer, more robust world.

Insects, especially insect pollinators, are important creatures worthy of appreciation and study. They are also in danger of dramatic population declines because of the changing climate, urbanization, and other anthropogenic factors. The good news is, we can all work together to protect insect pollinators. By planting attractive and pollinator-friendly gardens and being conscious of how you manage pests in your landscape, we can have a positive impact on our environment.

Now that you know all about the butterflies, beetles, and bees, among other interesting insects, you may see in your garden, we are going to discuss in more detail how you can design an area to be pollinator friendly. In the next chapter, we will discuss how knowing the preferences of different pollinators can help you decide where to plant your garden and, equally important, what to put in your garden to encourage the insect visitors you want to see flitting from flower to flower.

Pollination & Garden Design

Where Science and Art Meet

Pollination is an important and beneficial interaction between plants and the animals. At its most basic level, it's simply the transfer of pollen from flower to flower. Animals visit flowers seeking food in the form of nectar (sugar) and/or pollen (protein). During the foraging process, they transfer pollen grains among the blooms, ultimately enabling flowering plants to reproduce. The great majority of pollinators are insects, and of the vast number of insect pollinators, bees are the most well-known. There are other kinds of pollinators we have not discussed, such as lizards, hummingbirds, and some bat species, and while these are important in some specific cases, bees make up the majority of pollinating animals. Flies are the second most efficient pollinators, followed by everything else. Fortunately, bees, flies, butterflies, and other insects are easily enticed to visit your garden if you keep them in mind while designing and planting your pollinator haven.

How Plants Approach Pollination

In chapter 2, we discussed the kinds of insect pollinators and the types of plants they generally prefer. In this chapter we are going to dig a little more into the specifics of what makes a good pollinator plant and how you can group a bunch of these plants together to create a pollinator-friendly garden or landscape.

Flowering plants, also known as angiosperms, have been on this verdant earth for a long, long time. Their progenitors diverged from gymnosperms, flowerless plants that produce cones and seeds, in the Triassic Period (that was about 245 to 202 million years ago, in case you are trying to re-

Bees (left), thanks to their hairy bodies, are the most efficient pollinators, followed by flies (middle), which are the second most efficient. Butterflies (right), while beautiful, are inefficient pollinators.

member your geological history). Angiosperms are among the largest and most diverse groups within the kingdom Plantae and represent around 80 percent of all the known flowering plants in existence today.

It is because these remarkable plants are able to flower that they have adapted to a wide range of ecological niches. While plants do not need pollination in order to produce flowers, they do need pollination in order to maintain the genetic diversity that gives them a biological leg up and allows them to dominate terrestrial ecosystems. Pollination also ensures that a plant can robustly reproduce, produce seed, and, in many cases, develop adequate fruit to attract animals, which eat the fruit and subsequently disperse the seeds.

Anemophily: A Breezy Approach to Pollination

Some plants don't rely on insects or animals to spread their pollen; instead, they rely on the wind to blow pollen from one plant onto another. Anemophilous plants, plants that are pollinated by wind, are not the plants we typically think of when we imagine big, beautiful, eye-catching, bee-attracting posies. Their flowers typically have long stamens and pistils, and since they do not need to attract biotic (living) pollinators, they are usually dull colored and unscented, with small petals or even no petals at all, since no insect needs to land on them.

Anemophilous plants tend to produce abundant amounts of very light pollen, the better be

blown around; it's of low nutritional benefit to insects. Think of wheat, corn, oats, and brassicas like kale, cabbage, broccoli, and cauliflower. The original versions of these plants are not showy or scented, and although there are some exceptions, such as canola, by and large they don't attract bees. However, there are ornamental versions of these plants that have much fancier and more colorful foliage than their vegetable cousins. These ornamental brassicas are frequently grown as colorful landscape plants during the colder months in the South, and although you could eat them, they have been bred for looks, not flavor. Because these plants do not require (and therefore attract) pollinator insects, we do not recommend them for a pollinator garden.

Entomophily: Insect Pollination

Entomophilous ("insect-loving") plants have adapted especially for insect pollination. Pollinator insects and the plants they pollinate have coevolved to work together to complete the task of pollination (in the case of the plants) or food gathering (in the case of the pollinators). Entomophilous plants typically have characteristics that attract their pollinators. Their flowers may be brightly colored or release a scent that mimics insect pheromones. One classic example is the corpse flower: its blossoms smell like rotting flesh to attract dung beetles, flesh flies, and other carnivorous insects, which are the primary pollinators for this plant.

Insects such as butterflies and bees, on the other hand, have evolved to have physical adaptations for their role as pollinators. In order to facilitate the gathering of nectar, they have lapping or sucking mouthparts, or they have pollen baskets (called "corbiculae") on their hind legs for carrying pollen back to the hive. It is these attributes that determine which flowers the pollinators visit.

Clever Flowers Do It Best

Flowering plants have to be clever and work hard to ensure good pollination. In order to drive the exchange of genetic material and increase fecundity, they must lure pollinators with a complex array of attractions and cues—most commonly, they provide rewards of nectar, pollen, or other substances foragers desire. In some flowers, these rewards are easily accessible, but in others they can be obtained only by animals with specific behaviors or morphologies.

Sometimes the pollinating insect is not rewarded with anything other than perhaps frustration. One example that many plant lovers are familiar with the beautiful and diverse orchid family. Some orchids lure their pollinators through sexual deception: their flowers closely resemble female bees and attract male bees, which try to mate with them. Some orchid flowers deceive their pollinators by mimicking the scents produced by female insects. But no matter the mechanism, the male bees fly away frustrated: not only are there no female bees, but many orchids offer no nectar reward, either; it is all an elaborate hoax to trick insects into transferring pollen from one plant to the next.

Pollination in lady's slipper orchids (*Cypripedium* spp.) also involves deception and entrapment for unsuspecting insects, but these tactics tend to backfire in the long run. The flowers' bright colors are attractive, and the shape of the slipper part of the flower (the lip) encourages bees, flies, and beetles to crawl inside. The insects find no reward, however; instead, they are trapped, with a single exit through the ingeniously designed flower: they must crawl to the base of the lip, where they must pass the flower's stigma, in the process depositing any pollen they may have been carrying. Unfortunately for the orchids, bees tend to learn from this unsatisfying process and avoid future visits to these flowers, resulting in low pollination rates for lady's slipper orchids.

Another example of the synergism between plants and their pollinators—perhaps a more harmonious one than how orchids trick bees—is how nectar is stored within deep floral tubes in plants such as beardtongue, great blue lobelia (*Lobelia siphilitica*), and trumpet honeysuckle (*Lonicera sempervirens*). Generally, the nectar is accessible only to pollinators with mouthparts designed to take advantage of the depth of the floral structure that holds the nectar. In this case, long, tube-shaped flowers are most attractive to and frequented by hummingbirds and butterflies, which have long tongues perfectly designed for lapping up sweet nectar.

Different Flowers for Different Pollinators

It may seem obvious at this point that different flowers are adapted for pollination by different insects. Beetles are more likely to forage on plants with large, rounded, bowl-shaped flowers. Small bees, in contrast to medium and large bees, prefer small flowers that have broken outlines, such as goldenrods, golden Alexanders, and anise hyssop (*Agastache foeniculum*). Which pollinators are you especially interested in hosting in your garden? Your choice of plants will inform which insect visitors you have.

Easy-to-access bowl-shaped flowers generally have a prolific pollen ring in the middle of the flower. Plants with these kinds of flowers include St. John's wort (*Hypericum perforatum*, not native to the United States but not considered invasive) and eastern prickly pear (*Opuntia humifusa*). The flowers are used by all sorts of insects but especially honey bees, bumblebees, and certain solitary bees, which run around the inside of the flower to collect pollen on their bodies as efficiently as possible. Evening primrose (*Oenothera drummondii*), a bowl-shaped flower native to and common in the southern United States, attracts a large number of native bees but is also both a food and host plant for a number of butterfly species.

Plants in the parsley/carrot family (Apiaceae) feature small, flat, open flowers in bunches called umbels. One member of this family, Queen Anne's lace, also called wild carrot, is a common "weed" that was imported to the United States from Eurasia and is now widespread and easy to spot along roadsides and in cow pastures. Other common plants in this family are dill, parsley (*Petroselinum crispum*), chervil (*Anthriscus cerefolium*), and poison hemlock (*Conium maculatum*). (The first three are yummy in a salad, but the fourth is deadly!) These might not be plants you would ordinarily consider attractive in a pollinator paradise, but they are still attractive to pollinators. This is because the shallow flowers make the nectar easy to access, which appeals to insects with shorter tongues, such as hoverflies, small beetles, and small solitary bees, rather than to bumblebees or lepidopterans.

Fennel, another member of the parsley/carrot family, is a fragrant herb that is worthy of inclu-

sion in a pollinator garden. With feathery, fern-like leaves, it adds both color and texture to your garden and is an excellent host plant for swallow-tail butterfly larvae. If the voracious caterpillars leave you any fennel, you can harvest the leaves and toss them into your coleslaw, soups, or stews. Fennel flowers are also edible and make wonderful garnishes for your Fourth of July picnic dishes. Just don't plant fennel near dill plants—thanks to all the bees you will be hosting, cross pollination can occur, and the result will be strangely flavored seeds for both plants.

While you are in your garden making notes

Can Flowers Hear Bees?

Lilach Hadany and her team study what they call "phytoacoustics" ("plant sounds," an area of scientific study that leaves many scientists skeptical) in their lab at Tel Aviv University. In the first study of its kind, which has not yet been published in any scientific journal, they exposed evening primrose flowers to the sound of a flying bee and to synthetic sounds at similar frequencies and found that the flowers temporarily increased the sugar content in their nectar by 3 to 8 percent. Both the vibration and the nectar response were frequency specific: the flowers responded to sounds at the same frequencies as sounds made by pollinators but not to higher-frequency sounds. Hadany suggested that the bowl shape of these flowers might effectively act like ears, picking up the specific frequencies of bees' wings while tuning out irrelevant sounds like wind. The increased sugar concentration in the flowers' nectar is a reward that may draw in nearby bees, potentially increasing the chances of cross-pollination.

(opposite)
The more kinds of plants you have in your garden, the more kinds of pollinators and other wildlife will be drawn to your pollinator paradise. Shown here are a hoverfly on yarrow, a leafcutter bee on portulaca, and a gulf fritillary on a butterfly bush.

about the bees and butterflies you spot or harvesting your herbs, be sure to grab some long stems of fennel—they look great in fresh bouquets.

How Bees Approach Pollination

Generalists vs. Specialists

Even though there are more than 4,000 bee species in the United States, it is fairly easy to classify any bee you see into one of two very broad categories: generalists and specialists. Generalist bees account for about 80 percent of all bees flying around on any given day. As their name suggests, generalist bees forage on many different plant species, native and nonnative plants alike—essentially, they'll visit any suitable plant in bloom.

Some generalists, such as honey bees, tend to forage on a different species of flowering plant on each trip. Honey bees foraging on dandelions (*Taraxacum officinale*), for example, may work their way down the street or around the pasture, collecting pollen from all the dandelions in the area. Once their corbiculae are full, they head back to the hive, deposit their load, and head back out for another trip. This time, they'll likely focus not on dandelions but, perhaps, on redbuds, which are also host plants for nineteen species of butterflies and moths, including clouded sulphurs, luna moths, and spicebush swallowtails, or maybe on hawthorns (*Crataegus* spp.), an excellent early food source for bees and a large number of butterflies, moths, and other insects. Honey bees will visit any suitable flowers and may visit up to 5,000 flowers a day, so they cannot afford to be too picky.

Carpenter bees, whose genus name, *Xylocopa*, is Greek for "woodworker," are generalist bees that

Squash bees are found throughout much of the United States and Mexico, where they are important specialist pollinators of plants in the genus *Cucurbita*, including zucchini, yellow squash, pumpkins, and many gourds. By some estimates, squash bees alone may pollinate around two-thirds of the commercially grown squash in the United States. They are also often spotted visiting suburban vegetable gardens.

also demonstrate something scientists call "flower constancy." During the entire nest-preparation process, carpenter bees memorize the details of a single flower type and visit only that flower type. It is suspected that this constancy saves time during nest provisioning. Once the nest is complete, they go back to foraging on anything that strikes their fancy.

Around 770 bee species native to the eastern United States are considered specialist bees. These rely on just a handful of plant species or plants in a single family, and some bee species depend entirely on a single plant species. Perhaps the most well-known plant specialists are squash bees. Of these, the eastern cucurbit bee is widespread across the South and collects pollen only from—you guessed it—wild varieties and cultivars of squash plants.

Some *Hoplitis* bee species, named after the Hoplite soldiers of ancient Greece, visit only plants in the pea family (Fabaceae) or the borage family (Boraginaceae). Other *Hoplitis* species exclusively visit beardtongue.

The South, with its warm, humid climate, supports the greatest number of specialist bees in the United States. Original research published on bee associations showed that three of the five states that support the most specialist bees are in the South: North Carolina (139 species), Virginia (109 species), and Georgia (104 species). This same research reported that plants in the Asteraceae family support the greatest number of specialist bees with eighty-one dependent bee species. The plant genera associated with the greatest number of specialist bees are *Salix* (fourteen species), *Solidago* (twelve species), *Vaccinium* (eleven species), *Helianthus* (nine species), and *Symphyotrichum* (nine species).

The Foraging Trip

Many bees comb pollen that has collected on their body into small masses that they carry back to the hive on their rear legs in specially designed corbiculae. Most folks eschew this scientific term in favor of the common name, "pollen basket." After a bee visits a flower, she (because, remember, it is only the female bees that do the actual work) begins grooming herself and brushes the pollen down toward her hind legs and packs it into her pollen basket. A little nectar mixed with the pollen keeps it all together, and the hairs in the pollen basket hold it in place.

Some species of bees, such as leafcutter bees and mason bees, collect pollen on a hairy area

It is easy to spot the pollen basket (filled with the aster's orange pollen) on this worker honey bee.

under their abdomen called a "scopa" (also called the "pollen brush"). The corbicula and the scopa serve the same purpose: to safely hold pollen from hundreds of flowers for the return flight home.

Bees also collect nectar and have a special internal chamber called the honey stomach. This nectar is regurgitated when they get back to the nest. Some smaller species of solitary bees also ingest pollen and store it internally until they get back to the nest, where they regurgitate it in order to provision nest cells.

Into the Unknown

Despite the vast number and sheer diversity of bee species, it can be said that bees (and butterflies, ants, wasps, flies, and other insects) are searching for a few very basic things. When considering what pollinators need in order to survive, we can draw on our own experiences. Taking the human desire

for coffee and chocolate off the table (nooooo!), ultimately, humans and insects both need basically the same two things to sustain life: nutrients (including water, if we want to get super technical) and a place to live.

This is important to remember because we are getting ready to go deep into the weeds with details on garden size, plant texture, seasonality, and much more in order to help you envision, design, and plant a fabulous pollinator-friendly garden. In fact, we are going to share so much information, you may get overwhelmed. But have no fear as you venture forth to create your pollinator oasis: if you simply remember that bees and butterflies primarily need food and a place to live, you can plant anything you want, any place you want, in any order you want, as long as the plants you choose provide food and nesting space for pollinators. Whether to select specific plants to attract specific groups or species is up to you.

The rest of this book will help you design and establish a beautiful and resource-rich garden that will be the envy of your neighborhood. The inclusion of plants that provide pollen and nectar for pollinators will ensure that your artistically designed and sustainably planted garden will be full of pollinators.

Food and a Safe Place to Call Home

Nectar and Pollen

For bees, the two most important nutrients are carbohydrates and protein. Adult bees have never heard of the South Beach Diet and love themselves some carbs, which they require for energy and

Pollen has collected on the hairs on the back legs of this ligated furrow bee.

thermoregulation, and they get them in the form of sugars from nectar.

Bees get vital protein and fats from pollen. Although all bees need pollen at some stage in their lives, not all bees gather it; adult male bees have no use for pollen and therefore do not have pollen baskets. Adult female bees mostly eat nectar with a little pollen, though queens may consume more pollen, at least initially. Most of the pollen collected is mixed with a little nectar and stored as food for larvae.

Solitary bees feed pollen to their larvae. Honey bees differ in that the main consumers of pollen are nurse bees, young workers that digest pollen and produce jelly to feed to their brood.

When planning a bee-friendly garden, it's important to consider the difference between the quality and quantity of nectar and (especially) pol-

len. Mass-flowering crops, such as sunflower and canola, provide superabundant food for bees, but they tend to bloom for shorter periods of time. These crops also have the potential to increase bees' exposure to pesticides because they are both attractive to bees and are often planted around agricultural crops that are sprayed with chemicals (or are themselves sprayed).

Furthermore, for bees, foraging on huge fields of monoculture crops, whether sunflowers, almonds, or blueberries, leads to a nutritional imbalance. Pollen from multiple plant species is better because, like humans who eat a balanced diet, larvae who eat pollen foraged from multiple plant species are healthier in the long run than their monopollen-fed counterparts. In addition, certain amino acids are critical for developing larvae. Some pollen lacks essential amino acids or has the wrong proportions of amino acids for developing larvae. So, again, a mixed-pollen diet is much better than pollen from a single source.

Home Sweet Home

Another very important element of a pollinator-friendly garden is a safe place for pollinators to rest and, perhaps most importantly, to rear young. Like humans who prefer rural life to urban life, or vice versa, different bees prefer different niches in which to place their homes. Unlike our beloved managed honey bees, which live presumably happy lives in social hives in wooden boxes or hollow trees, with many sisters working diligently, native bees are solitary (the bee version of misanthropes, if you will) and have different needs for their homes.

Since solitary bees typically build a new individual nest every year, they utilize different types

It is not uncommon to see stingless ground-nesting bees making nests like these in backyards with sunny south-facing slopes. While they're solitary, they tend to group their nests together.

ing through the garden, which allows undisturbed space for ground-nesting bees.

Garden Design Basics

Combining What You Want with What Bees Need

While bees and humans generally desire similar elements in a garden, it's for different reasons: humans are thinking about aesthetics and what looks good, while bees are looking for easy access to pollen and nectar. Humans typically want lots of color and variety in the garden, and as much color as possible for as much of the year as possible. While bees do not select which flowers they visit by their beauty, we can still use this human preference to their advantage. By planting flowers that bloom for longer periods of time or selecting plants with different bloom times, we can provide pollinators with pollen and nectar for as much of the year as possible. And selecting plants for variety and a range of colors meets pollinators' nutritional need for floral diversity. Our desire for plant species diversity in a "gardenscape" also allows it to be utilized by a wider variety of pollinators.

Color

In a word, *color* is the name of the game for a pollinator garden. Plants that are pollinated by wind tend to not be colorful at all, since they don't need to attract insects. Bee-pollinated flowers are usually blue or yellow; they're generally not red because in bees' ultraviolet vision, red appears black. However, no single color is better at attracting pollinators—just the fact that a flower is colorful is enough. More specifically, it's important for flow-

of structures and a variety of materials. Approximately 70 percent of wild bees dig holes in the ground to lay their eggs; others nest in grass stems, wood, and even in stone piles.

When planning your pollinator-friendly space, be creative in allowing for bare earth, which encourages native bees to make nests. For example, rather than a heavily mulched path, you could have some small pavers or stepping-stones wind-

BEES AND HUMANS BOTH WANT PLANT DIVERSITY

For the bees, plant diversity means...	For the humans, plant diversity means...
Many food opportunities for different kinds of bees	A more dynamic, aesthetically pleasing garden
More and better nutrition	Lots of color
Flowers of all shapes and sizes to supports a range of bee tongue sizes	More drama
A long period of available food and habitat throughout the year	A showy garden during a large part of the year

ers to have a high contrast between flower parts (petals, sepals, stamens, and anthers). With their ultraviolet vision, bees see foliage as dull grays and flowers as more vivid grays. A human may just see a flower as yellow, but often there is a high contrast between the petals and the flower throat or other parts, which bees see as runway lights of sorts—these are often referred to as "nectar guides."

Flowers pollinated by beetles tend to be white or dull; flies seem to prefer dull red and brown colors (although, truth be told, they are flies are also guided by flower smell). Moths are attracted to flowers that are white or yellow because they stand out in the dwindling light of dusk, when moths become active. Although hummingbirds are not primary pollinators, humans often try to attract them to their gardens. Hummingbirds are drawn to bright red or yellow flowers that are large and tubular. But this is not a hard-and-fast rule, since hummingbirds forgot to read the book that says they prefer red flowers. Often it depends on what food sources are available and how hungry a hummingbird is. We often see hummingbirds around our purple salvia (*Salvia* spp.). Even though the

blossoms are not red, salvia still produces sweet, sweet nectar, making it a fantastic plant for hummingbirds. Other good nectar plants for hummingbirds include red buckeye (*Aesculus pavia*), columbine, and cardinal flower (*Lobelia cardinalis*).

Color is the garden design element that resonates most strongly with humans. We love our garden drama. When it comes to individuals, color preferences are extremely personal. We will get more into this in chapter 4, when we tackle how to design a pollinator garden.

Garden Size

Any size garden will do. We are always amazed at how just one well-chosen, newly planted perennial will attract pollinators immediately. For example, Anne has a single blue hyssop (*Agastache* × 'Blue Fortune') along her front walkway in and among other perennials, and it is always the one most covered in pollinators. On any given day, there will be numerous species all over it, commingling, not caring one bit about any human who might be walking up the path or weeding beneath the plant. So even if you have just a small patch available for planting, a few plants could be beneficial for pollinators. Even one pollinator-friendly plant is better than none.

But if you have the space, to be as helpful for the environment as possible, it's better to dedicate more space to pollinator plants. Bees that target one specific plant species per flight, or series of flights, will benefit from having multiple plants of a single species to facilitate efficient foraging. These ladies certainly appreciate plant masses (groupings) and/or repeated plant species. You may have come across sources in the past that recommend specific numbers, like this: "Masses should be a minimum of three feet by three feet and should include a minimum of fifteen plant species." These recommendations are not supported by any research we found; they are, however, a logical place to start. Different bee species will be flying in your garden at any one time, each has different sustenance needs, and each requires flowers of different sizes and shapes. Having just one pollinator-friendly plant per season is less than ideal, so in general, the more plants and more species you include, the better.

Often general recommendations do not take context into consideration. The pollinator garden you create is not the be-all and end-all of habitats. Pollinators will be visiting plants outside of your garden. Consider your yard or garden a way station. Many pollinators will visit for a bit and then move on to another location. With any luck, they will be back for more soon.

Garden Style: Formal or Informal?

While bees will not care if your garden is formal (symmetrical and full of straight lines) or informal (asymmetrical, with curvy bed lines), it's import-

Even though insect pollinators and mammals see flowers very differently, having colorful plants in your garden will please both you and your pollinator friends, such as these bumblebees. While this salvia looks blue to humans, it will be a shade of gray for the bee—its favorite!

At top is a plan for an informal garden, asymmetrical and featuring curvilinear beds. At bottom is a plan for a formal garden, symmetrical and featuring straight lines.

garden center, she selects whatever catches her fancy. As a result, her garden is a random assortment of plants stuck into areas where another plant died or was cut back. Anne, when being extremely generous, refers to that as an informal planting approach. The term "informal" can also refer to the garden layout and simply mean that the lines of your garden are curvilinear and asymmetrical, not necessarily that plants aren't arranged or chosen for specific locations.

A formal approach is a completely planned green space that demonstrates humanity's dominion over nature. Formal gardens rely on straight lines and geometric shapes, such as squares and triangles, and they usually have a profusion of green, leafy plants instead of flowers. Hedges are commonly used in formal gardens to create geometric shapes and to define paths. In general, the formal style is higher management because it requires more inputs—your time, energy, materials, money—to keep it looking so tidy.

Perennial borders can be formal, informal, or a combination (for example, a wild-looking perennial border framed by a low evergreen hedge) depending on the plants you select. But formality is perhaps a less important consideration when planting a border than layering and seasonality. A properly designed border is a masterpiece of juxtaposed shapes, colors, and textures. For example, the upright stalks of red hot poker (*Kniphofia uvaria*) and the tall blue blooms of blue hyssop add vertical interest to a bed packed with the cloudlike pink sedum (*Hylotelephium spectabile*) and purple coneflower. Plus, the sturdy and compact perennials will help support the taller plants as they grow.

When contemplating your pollinator garden, it

ant to consider these elements when determining your personal garden style. At one extreme, absolute formality in a landscape reduces all natural elements to stern geometric shapes. On the other end of the spectrum is absolute informality, which may look like complete randomness, as if no hand has imposed any sort of human order.

Danesha's planting style is what we like to refer to as "yes, please." When she goes to a nursery or

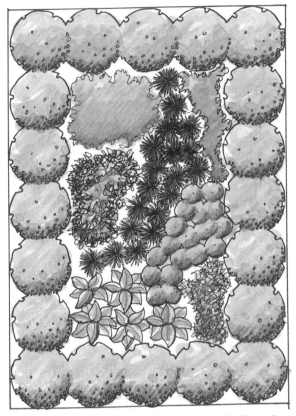

This plan combines features of formal and informal gardens.

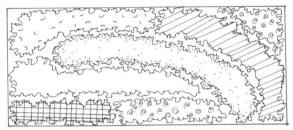

At top are more traditional perennial masses; at bottom are masses more like those designed by Gertrude Jekyll. These thinner, more linear masses are woven together so that no matter the season, there is never a gap without visual interest.

Perennial Masses and Sweeps

Many pollinator gardens rely on perennials for the lion's share of pollen- and nectar-providing plants. A very traditional way of planting perennials is to group them in larger masses, often called "sweeps." We will discuss diversifying your plant palette a bit later, but since perennials are used so heavily, we need to address some design considerations here.

British designer Gertrude Jekyll was famous for her perennial borders. Her color groupings; variety of plant forms, leaf forms, and textures; and wave after wave of seasonal interest have inspired gardeners and designers for a century. The key to creating perennial borders like Jekyll's is to layer the masses so that when one perennial is done with its flower show, the declining foliage and its eventual

might be more reasonable to think of a style that falls somewhere between the extremes formal and informal and perhaps combines elements of each. There is no right or wrong way to strike a balance between the formal and the informal approaches. The successful choice is the one that adds bee-welcoming plants in a way that suits both the setting and your personal style.

absence go unnoticed because other plants have taken over the show in front and behind the first species. Instead of planting large masses, Jekyll tended to weave thinner, linear masses together so that a single species mass that either had yet to emerge or was already past did not leave a gaping hole in the border. Not only does this look better, but it also ensures that bees are never without a food supply. Thinking through a garden's seasonality very carefully will be a huge benefit to pollinators as well as human enjoyment.

Sweeps vs. Varied Plantings

Historically, planting design in the southern United States has favored sweeps. While this is great for honey bees, which typically visit one plant species per flight (this makes for easier and more efficient foraging), a space occupied by one plant species has limited seasonality. Once a flower has completed its show, there is little of interest in that space.

Landscape designers and homeowners must rely on placing masses of different plant species adjacent to each other to ensure seasonality and diversity. The trick to a well-designed planting of massed perennials is to keep the masses skinny and have them intertwine, or at least "hug" one another, just a bit.

For plants that act as host plants for butterfly larvae, keep in mind that they are typically eaten down to the ground by the caterpillars at some point. If you do not want naked stems in the forefront of your garden, tuck these delicious host plants in a less noticeable location in your garden or yard.

A recent trend in planting design has been a shift to meadow-type planting. With this approach, the planting looks more random and seems a bit chaotic, but an incredible amount of layering can happen in one place. Additionally, because there is a great diversity of plants occupying a space, there is less opportunity for weeds to take hold—always a bonus as far as we are concerned.

Stand-Alone vs. Embedded Pollinator Habitats

A pollinator habitat can be a stand-alone garden (perhaps an island bed between the sidewalk and house or a very small patch of flowers around a mailbox), or it can be incorporated into preexisting garden beds. A stand-alone garden can be a wonderful way for novice gardeners to build knowledge and confidence. A planting bed around a mailbox removes the frustration of having to mow around the post on a weekly basis. A downside is that it might be harder to water, especially the farther from the house (and hose spigot) it is.

An embedded pollinator garden is one that is part of already-established planting beds that may also include plants that don't function as pollinator habitat—and that's okay! Here's an example: Perhaps you have some established evergreen foundation shrubs (right along the front of your house). You could extend the bed outward, creating more garden space, and work in more layers of different-size plants, some deciduous shrubs for added seasonal interest, and some pollinator plants for color. From this small project, you've increased curb appeal and human happiness, and provided more pollen and nectar for bees. It's a win-win-win.

Your pollinator garden may be part of an existing garden, as in the picture at left, where plants like coneflowers were added to a perennial border to attract pollinators. Or you may create a whole new space for a pollinator garden, as in the picture at right, where a dedicated pollinator garden was created.

Ensuring Seasonality

Bees start to emerge from their nests when temperatures reach around 57°F, usually in the early spring. We need to provide plants they can use for food from then until late fall, when they head into their nests to stay for the winter.

It is helpful to do some research on seasonal plants ahead of time and visit a garden center with a list in hand, so that you select plants for all seasons and bloom times. Yes, it's good to see what the plants look like in person, but when you're there, you will be likely drawn to whatever is flowering that day instead of planning for the whole year. The lists and examples in the next chapter can help you get started.

The easiest way to ensure seasonality is by charting flowering times when you are designing your garden. Create a phenological (bloom time) chart that includes start and end times of bloom for each plant. At the very least, include columns for spring,

This sketch shows one way of incorporating a stand-alone pollinator garden. The coneflowers in the center will attract pollinators, while the ornamental grasses on the right will provide nesting for some native bees and winter interest for humans. The planting bed incorporates the mailbox. Won't your mail carrier be pleased? And you'll no longer have to trim the grass around the post.

summer, fall, and winter, but the more specific you can be, the better. Simply expanding your columns to include early to mid spring, mid to late spring, early to mid summer, and so forth, will help you be more precise. The ultimate flowering chart includes columns for each month. Flowering times vary in the Southeast, from the southern regions to the northern and from low-elevation coastal areas to the high elevation of the mountains, so it's best to create your own phenological chart for your area. You can use your garden journal or the margins of this book for this purpose, or even create a spreadsheet.

Phenological charts typically document flower bloom for pollen and nectar. But you can and should also include plants that provide winter benefits, such as dormant ornamental grasses with hollow stems, which bees may nest in, and spent flower heads with seeds that provide food for wildlife. These charts should also document what is evergreen, since it is always lovely to see some green in the winter.

Size Matters—Tongue Size, That Is

Most bees possess a fairly rigid hollow tube through which they can suck nectar. This is usually called a proboscis in lepidopterans, but in other insects it's often referred to informally as a "tongue." A pollinator's tongue length closely dictates the shape and size of flowers that it can utilize because the floral nectary (location of the nectar) is usually deep inside the flower, and the pollinator has to be able to reach it.

Tongue length varies between one and nineteen millimeters. While honey bees have a short-to-medium tongue length of about six millimeters, bumblebees have longer tongues. Butterflies and hummingbirds have the longest tongues. Each species, then, can benefit from flowers of different sizes and shapes. This underscores the importance of planting a variety of flowers—not only because humans love variety, but because it is important to have plant diversity in order to support all the bees and beneficial pollinators in your garden.

Only bumblebees, butterflies, and some moths have tongues long enough to reach the floral nectary of many flowers, so only these insects can pollinate these flowers. Plants with tubular flower

SIMPLE PHENOLOGICAL CHART

| | Visual Interest | | | |
Plant	Spring	Summer	Fall	Winter
Eastern redbud (*Cercis canadensis*)	▓			
Purple coneflower (*Echinacea purpurea*)		▓		
Dwarf fothergilla (*Fothergilla gardenii*)	▓		▓	
Trumpet honeysuckle (*Lonicera sempervirens*)	▓	▓	▓	▓
Rosemary (*Salvia rosmarinus*)	▓	▒	▓	▓

DETAILED PHENOLOGICAL CHART

| | Visual Interest | | | | | | | | | | | |
Plant	Jan	Feb	Mar	Apr	May	Jun	Jul	Aug	Sep	Oct	Nov	Dec
Eastern redbud (*Cercis canadensis*)				▒								
Purple coneflower (*Echinacea purpurea*)				▒	▒	▒	▒	▒	▒			
Dwarf fothergilla (*Fothergilla gardenii*)				▒						▒		
Trumpet honeysuckle (*Lonicera sempervirens*)	▓	▓	▓	▒	▓	▓	▓	▓	▓	▓	▓	▓
Rosemary (*Salvia rosmarinus*)	▓	▓	▓	▓	▒	▒	▓	▓	▓	▓	▓	▓

▒ flowers   ▓ foliage

shapes are particularly appealing to long-tongued insects and hummingbirds, whose very long, specialized beaks are well adapted to extracting nectar from deep inside flowers. These plants also depend on these pollinators for pollination, so, as we have said before, it is good to have multiple options in your garden.

Good plant choices for attracting and supporting butterflies and hummingbirds include the following:

* **Fuchsia** (*Fuchsia* spp., tender perennial): The reddish fuchsia flowers tolerate heat better than flowers of other colors and are popular with hummingbirds. Well suited for USDA hardiness zones 10 and 11, fuchsia bears bright, pendent blooms in solid and bicolor shades of white, pink, red, fuchsia, and purple. Fuchsias bloom throughout the spring and into the fall and stay evergreen in frost-free zones. In cold climates, bring the plants indoors before the first fall frost.
* **Bleeding heart** (*Lamprocapnos spectabilis*, perennial): This plant's airy green foliage provides a striking backdrop to the pink-and-white pendent flowers. Bleeding heart grows up to three feet tall and is ideally suited to partial to full shade with well-drained, moist soil high in organic matter. Bleeding heart flowers bloom in early spring in USDA zones 3 through 9, then slip into dormancy during the summer's heat.
* **Turk's cap lily** (*Lilium superbum*, perennial): The plant grows up to seven feet tall in moist soil and partial or full sun. A single stalk bears multiple large, orange flowers. Hardy in USDA zones 4 through 7, this lily grows from a bulb, and the leaves turn yellow and die after the flowers bloom. Do not cut the foliage until it is brown, as the leaves feed the bulb for the next year's bloom.
* **Comfrey** (*Symphytum officinale*, perennial): A very hardy perennial, this plant is great for the back of a herbaceous border. It has a very long flowering period, from May to August, and is one of the very best plants for bees. It's visited by both long- and short-tongued species, the latter often robbing nectar from holes bitten in the tops of the flowers. Comfrey can be chopped down regularly and used to make excellent compost. It can grow anywhere from one to three feet high and can smother smaller plants nearby.

Plants and flowers good for short-tongued native bees include these:

* **Asters** (perennial): The pinks, blues, and purples of late-summer and fall aster flowers are a delight to all bees. There are so many wonderful varieties to choose from, it is hard to know where to start. Some species are wonderful late-fall bloomers with lavender-blue flowers and orange centers, while others are more bluish and bloom a bit earlier. They have the tendency to sprawl, so give them quite a bit of room to grow.
* **Black-eyed Susans** (*Rudbeckia* spp., annual or perennial): Nothing says summer like a beautiful patch of black-eyed Susans, and bees appreciate their prolific flowers just as much as we do.

All kinds of social and solitary bees feed on comfrey, whose flowers refill with nectar approximately every 45 minutes. Who says there is no free lunch?

These flowers are all well-suited for short-tongued bees. Clockwise from top left: black-eyed Susans, asters, sedum, and blanketflowers.

- **Cosmos** (*Cosmos bipinnatus*, annual): These are a favorite of honey bees and native bees alike. They thrive in many regions and are among the easiest flowers to grow from seeds. Plus, they are generous reseeders!
- **Coneflowers** (perennial): Bright and colorful, these blooms are daisylike and have raised centers. Their flowers are nectar rich, and the seeds found in the dried flower heads also attract birds, especially goldfinches. They tend to bloom midsummer and tolerate drought and heat relatively well. Coneflowers also make great cut flowers.
- **Sedum** (*Sedum* spp., perennial): Sedum's common name, stonecrop, is indicative of its toughness. Leaf colors include light green, blue-green, gray-green, variegated green-and-white, and dark maroon. Flowers may be white or shades of pink or yellow. They tend to bloom in late summer, which provides a bountiful option for bees and butterflies alike.

Selecting Nourishing Cultivars

It is easier to create a list of plants that are beneficial for pollinators than one might think. In general, if the plant produces nectar or pollen, some pollinator will find it and use it as a food source. However, when you're planting to aid in the nutrition of bees and other pollinating insects, it is important to avoid some specific types of plants. For pollinators, not all pollen is created equal, and not all pollen provides the nutrition bee larvae need to grow and be healthy. Day lily is a good example, and if you watch, you will not see bees or other pollinators visiting these flowers. While we advocate for planting both native plants and well-behaved

Rattlesnake master, a member of the parsley/carrot family native to the South, is a huge hit with pollinators of all kinds. Beetles, bees, and moths of all varieties use this plant as forage, and Heather Holm's fantastic book *Pollinators of Native Plants* documents 11 types of wasps who visit it. If you were to plant only a single plant for pollinators, this might be the one to choose.

What We Mean When We Talk about Plants

Plant origins can be a bit confusing, so here are a few definitions to help you when you're at a garden center or nursery:

Straight species—The original, naturally occurring form of a plant

Variety—A naturally occurring variation of a species

Cultivar—A plant that has been bred for specific characteristics (the name is a mash-up of "cultivated" and "variety")

Native species—A plant that was naturally occurring in an area before it was settled by people

Nativar—A cultivar of a native plant. Some native-plant purists don't recognize nativars as true native plants. The nativars are often popular and more frequently cultivated, and a bit easier to find than the original species.

Invasive species—A plant species that spreads much more than you want it to, by way of seeds, root runners, or colonizing/thicket-forming tendencies. Some folks equate "invasive" with "introduced," but there are many well-behaved introduced plants (the South's beloved crape myrtle, for example, which is not especially good for bees but is a prolific bloomer and part of the quintessential look of our southern streets), and there are native plants that are invasive when it comes to home gardens (northern sea oats is a great example).

introduced species, use caution when selecting plant cultivars to make sure they're actually nutritious for pollinators.

Unfortunately, not all cultivars offer the same nutritional benefits. Some are bred for new and exciting colors, or for double blooms or flower shape, and others are bred for pest resistance. Purple coneflower, one of our favorite pollinator-friendly plants, has been bred into scores of cultivars that have all manner of colors, double blooms, and so on, but many of these cultivars produce less pollen, and/or their pollen is inaccessible because of extra whorls of petals. Ninebark (*Physocarpus* spp.) is beneficial for pollinators and widely sold as a native shrub. However, this easy-to-grow, acidic-soil-loving deciduous shrub has been bred into dozens of cultivars that feature unusual or showy foliage that's not good for all insects. The foliage of the red-leaved cultivars, for example, is high in anthocyanins, which may be toxic to caterpillars or other insects.

The Xerces Society for Invertebrate Conserva-

While beautiful, many dahlia cultivars are unable to produce pollen and therefore make poor pollinator forage.

tion speculates that the pollen in cultivars often has reduced nutritional benefits, which could harm pollinators who rely on them. This is likely true in some cultivars, but unfortunately, it has not been well studied, so there is virtually no information on which highly cultivated plants have good-quality pollen and which do not. We can also point to many cultivars that bees absolutely love (blue hyssop 'Blue Fortune', 'Forest Pansy' redbud, and 'Flamethrower' orange coneflowers come to mind). But is the pollen quality the same as (or close to) the original's? Or is the pollen lacking nutrition, but the nectar is particularly tasty? At this point, researchers do not have a definite answer. The bottom line is that if you can get your hands on the straight species (the original species from which cultivars are bred), you'll likely provide higher-quality, more-accessible pollen for pollinators.

Here's our best guideline: avoid using flowers that have multiple whorls of petals (often called "doubles"). Highly bred cultivars are much more likely to have doubles than their straight species counterparts. Plants with the words "flore pleno" should ring warning bells; the term means "with a full flower" and will almost certainly mean the plant is a double. Floral nectaries are much easier to access in single flowers than in doubles because the change in the flower's anatomy (from single to double) makes the nectar more difficult to access and reduces the amount of pollen produced. Ergo, these flowers make lousy pollinator forage.

Even though increasing pollinator habitats has gained rapidly in importance in recent years, the recent landscape trend has been for breeders and designers to use the showier double-flower culti-

VARIETIES THAT ARE GOOD FOR BEES AS SINGLES BUT NOT DOUBLES

Plant	Single-flower forms that are good for bees	Double-flower cultivars that aren't helpful for bees
Hawthorn (*Crataeagus laevigata*)	Straight species	'Paul's Scarlet'
Japanese anemones (*Anemone* × *hybrida*)	'Honorine Jobert', 'September Charm', 'Pretty Lady', 'Lucky Charm'	'Margarete', 'Whirlwind'
Avens (*Geum* spp.)	'Mrs. J. Bradshaw'	'Lady Stratheden'
Cinquefoil (*Potentilla reptans*)	Straight species	'Pleniflora'
Purple coneflower (*Echinacea purpurea*)	Straight species, 'Magnus', 'White Swan', PowWow series	Supreme series, Double Scoop series, Cone-fections series
Rose of Sharon (*Hibiscus syriacus*)	Straight species, 'Minerva', 'Purple Pillar', 'Bluebird'	Chiffon series, 'Lucy'

vars in landscapes, and therefore we see more and more of them in our public spaces and garden catalogs. The fact that plant breeding has followed the demand of gardeners makes simple economic sense, but from a biodiversity standpoint, it's an undesirable trend. The question is, can garden designers influence public taste sufficiently for nurseries to change their ways, or would not using double-flower cultivars put the breeders and nurseries out of a job? We do not presume to answer this complex question, but we do encourage you, as a bee-friendly gardener, to carefully consider all these issues as you select plants for your pollinator haven.

Small Creatures, Complex Bee-havior

You do not have to be an expert in insect behavior to appreciate and study how the behavior of pollinators influences garden design and plant selection. Knowing even a little about how beneficial insects, such as bees, behave can help you make decisions about what you need and want in your garden.

Like humans, bees are subject to external pressures that may change their behavior. Sometimes these pressures are applied intentionally: sometimes we feed bees in a laboratory chemicals or stimulants to see how their behavior changes. While this may seem unusual or even cruel, it can in help us better understand how human medications may support immune responses, how chemicals may affect human memory, and how drug addiction affects the human brain.

Bees don't always do exactly what we expect and seek out plants that provide the best nutrition. Recently scientists discovered the reason behind one example of this behavior, in the process challenging our previous understanding of what makes for a good bee forage plant. As pollinator scientists, we generally agree that plants that produce pollen that is high in protein are good for bees, while plants that produce low-quality or protein-poor pollen are not. But wait! Nature does not like us to get too comfortable in our knowledge, and we are learning that this may not be as straightforward as we thought. Sunflowers are typically thought of as low-quality forage for bees because their pollen is protein poor. While this is true, recent research in bee health has demonstrated that the bees you see feeding busily on sunflowers know something we scientists did not. Sunflower pollen, though protein poor, helps bees become resistant to pathogens.

Here's another favorite example of how bees preferentially visit plants that provide some benefit other than good nutrition: bees often visit certain plants that produce caffeine in their nectar. Caffeine is naturally produced in these plants as a defense chemical to deter harmful insects and lure pollinators. Just as caffeine allows us to transform from figurative zombies in the mornings to good worker bees, it also acts as a stimulant and potential memory enhancer in bees who feed on the nectar. It appears to increase bees' ability to remember where the flower with the caffeine-containing nectar is, thus increasing the chances of a return visit.

While caffeine makes bees work more efficiently,

Sunflowers Keep Bees Healthy

Sunflower pollen is generally considered to be poor bee forage because it's low in protein and lacks some amino acids. However, research done at North Carolina State University by R. Irwin and her laboratory team showed that when bumblebees and honey bees were fed a diet of sunflower pollen, they had dramatically lower rates of infection by certain pathogens. Bumblebees on the sunflower diet also had generally better colony health than bees fed on other flower pollen. This is good news for beekeepers and other sunflower lovers because it confirms that sunflowers are a worthy addition to a pollinator-friendly garden.

cocaine turns them into big fat liars. When scientists fed cocaine to honey bees in a laboratory, they found that the bees reacted to the stimulant much as humans do: cocaine altered their judgment, stimulated their behavior, and made them overly enthusiastic about things that might not otherwise excite them. For example, honey bees "dance" to communicate—specifically, through dance they give their fellow bees directions to good food. But honey bees high on cocaine exaggerate their moves and overemphasize the food's quality.

We are not suggesting that you put a caffeine- or cocaine-producing plant in your garden, but it is important to remember that plants (and flowers) bring more resources to the garden than simply nectar or high-protein pollen. Choose plants that you like, and it is likely that the pollinators will find reasons to use them as well. They may have benefits for bees we don't know about yet.

One Size Does Not Fit All

In terms of pollinator preferences and plant delights, it is not a case of "one size fits all"—different bees like different plants for different reasons. This is a great reason to select and plant a wide range of flowers in your garden. Understanding a little bit about the biology of bees, beetles, and butterflies will help you determine the characteristics or types of flowers you want to have in your pollinator garden. It may also help you be more selective when you receive the first garden catalog in the mail in January and are tempted to buy every single one of their pollinator-friendly plants.

Step away from those garden catalogs, but be sure you have your garden journal handy. By now you should have an idea of the general types of insects you want to entice into your nectar- and pollen-rich landscape, and you may have even identified your favorite pollinator (that's right, we all have one, and it is okay to admit it), as well as the best types of flowers to draw it in. The next step is to take your thoughts about flowers, color, sweeps, and seasonality, and turn this hot mess into a beautifully conceived garden design. How do you do that? We're glad you asked. In chapter 4, we will help you become a garden designer extraordinaire.

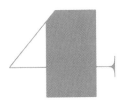

Designing a Habitat to Support Pollinators

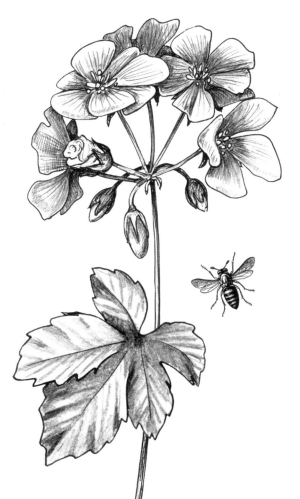

We cannot stress enough how critical it is to create more pollinator habitats with new and existing landscapes. Remember, any additional habitat is a necessary and helpful habitat. Some people might think that small gardens cannot have much impact, but that is simply not the case. Even a few plants can make a difference. Residential gardens might seem less important than public sites because they're smaller, but home gardens are, in fact, quite vital for increasing pollinator habitat. Research has shown that residential gardens are more ecologically diverse than, for example, many natural areas and larger designed spaces, because they are purposely created to have more drama and more flowers than would be seen in nature. They are often showier and more biologically diverse, and have more seasonality incorporated into the landscape. On top of all that, a residential garden is installed fairly quickly after a design is created, so the time from design ideas to a paper plan to an installed garden is often relatively short.

We are always amazed to see how quickly the pollinators appear after plant installation. In the case of one student-led installation on the student center's green roof at North Carolina State University, we had bees visiting our giant hyssop immediately after planting. How did they know how to find our garden, five floors up, and in a space where there had previously been absolutely no plants? Who knows! But they did. A human-built, small-scale garden can have a substantial impact rather quickly.

Home gardens are especially important because of their impact in aggregate. There are over 40 million acres of turf in the United States—that's roughly the size of Texas. Turfgrass provides no ecological benefit. Imagine if we reduced the amount of turfgrass in our yards (the parts we are not using for children's play, dogs' romping, and entertaining) and converted it to gloriously beautiful pollinator habitat. All those improved yards added together would be substantial. Further, what one homeowner does in his or her yard can influence what happens in neighboring yards. Researchers have tracked how garden elements incorporated on one property end up spreading throughout the neighborhood (figuratively, not literally—we hope). Your pollinator-friendly project could be an inspiration for others.

Now, how to begin creating your pollinator oasis? It might seem a little overwhelming at first, so let's break the process down and tackle each step one at a time. This chapter starts with larger design issues such as garden context, site selection, and other concepts, then explores the smaller details, such as plant selection and how to put combinations of plants together.

Garden Context: Considering Use and Experience

Take stock of the area where you are planning to create a pollinator habitat. Since it will be lovely, you'll want to enjoy it along with the bees and butterflies, so placement is important. Two good locations for a pollinator habitat are in line with views from major windows or adjacent to a patio, but the possibilities are virtually limitless. Other ideal locations might be along a path or near your mailbox. Any of these places are fine; you just want to be deliberate in your approach.

Next, consider how you and others will experi-

ence this garden. Will you be gazing at it from a window in the comfort of your air-conditioned living room during the July heat and humidity? (We do this too. We call it "armchair gardening.") Will the garden be seen by people walking by with their kiddos in a stroller or zipping by on bicycles? Is your garden best viewed while sitting on a bench in the garden? The answers to these questions can guide the kind of planting scheme you adopt. A garden viewed while passing by swiftly has more impact if there is a greater quantity of fewer species. Think of highway plantings by your local Department of Transportation—they often use thousands of plants from a single flower species to wow drivers speeding by at sixty-five miles per hour. These single-species plantings have greater impact because of the large massed planting and the short period of time drivers have to appreciate them. However, if you or someone else will enjoy the garden while sitting on a nearby bench, then the planting should engage the viewer by providing them with a variety of plants to hold their interest for a spell. Taller plants with larger flowers and foliage will be seen better from a distance. Smaller plants with daintier flowers and leaves are better seen up close and personal.

Garden Placement

Let There Be Light

Most pollinator plants prefer sun, so a full-sun or part-sun location is ideal. A sunny location also does double duty in attracting pollinators because most bees prefer the warmth of the sun. Larger trees may provide too much shade for plants to grow well and competes with them for nutrients

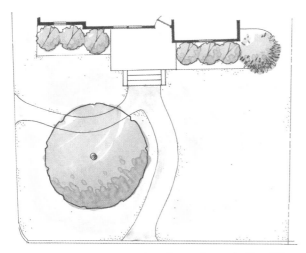

This typical front yard plan shows the majority of the yard in turf. The foundation plantings provide little food or cover for pollinators.

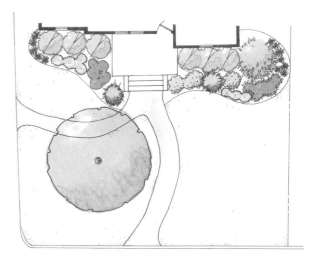

This plan expands the one at left by adding layered plantings in front of existing foundation plants. The increased diversity of plants is good for pollinators, adds curb appeal, and reduces the amount of high-maintenance turf.

and water. Anyone who has tried to start a new garden under large trees has experienced these challenges.

By "full sun," we mean the garden receives six or more hours of sun per day. "Part sun" means it gets fewer than six hours of sun, and likely receives a bit of shade from a structure or other plants for part of that time. Do not despair if you do not have full sun. Pollinators will still visit plants in part shade, but the diversity of the visitors will be reduced.

Using Your Front Yard

A front yard affords unique opportunities and challenges for a new pollinator-friendly garden. Many front yards consist of turf and minimal foundation plantings, and perhaps a tree or two. If the turf is not used for play or entertaining space, consider reducing its square footage. It is a monoculture

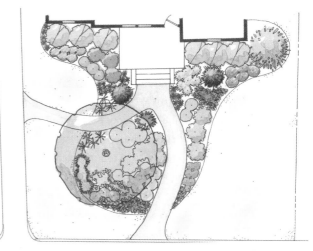

This final front yard plan reduces the amount of turf even more while adding significantly more plant species and drama. Notice how the plants in the first and second scheme are still in place, making this design easy to phase in over time as budget and energy allow.

that invites unbalanced ecology and can require a lot of management and resources. Some homeowners want to remove all the turf in their yard. The issue for most homeowners is that although turf is generally thought of as high maintenance, most people have some knowledge of how to manage it. A little fertilizer in the spring, regular mowing in the summer, and done! Replacing turf with something else, such as shrubs or flowers, can be overwhelming, especially for homeowners who are struggling with knowing which plants are which, let alone how to take care of them.

Perhaps a more realistic goal is to reduce the amount of turf and use some of its square footage for a glorious pollinator habitat. That way, lawn is minimized and more pollinator-friendly plants are incorporated into your landscape. And chances are, as long as you keep some turf, you won't ruffle the feathers of your homeowners' association (HOA) if you have one.

Let's All Just Get Along

If you live in a neighborhood with an active HOA, the amount of turf you can effectively replace with pollinator habitat may be limited—not that HOAs are against pollinators, but they often want the neighborhood to have a consistent look. Even if your neighborhood does not have an HOA, it is a good idea to consider what your neighbors are doing in *their* yards. If there are green lawns on either side of the meadow you would like in your front yard, how well will that be accepted? It is better to have a conversation with your neighbors— always a good policy—and lay the groundwork for what you intend. This is especially true if you are making dramatic changes to your yard, such as re-

At Anne's property, the most-visited flowers, mountain mint, comfrey, and vervain, are planted on the interior of her beds, so passersby aren't alarmed by the numerous pollinators flying around. The hot pink flowers and silver-foliaged perennial in the photo is rose campion, supposedly attractive to butterflies, but she's never spied any on them.

Keeping the Peace

Native bees typically do not sting because they are not aggressive and, unlike honey bees, do not stick around to defend their young. Honey bees, however, may sting to protect their family. When deciding where to place a honey bee hive, think carefully about the landscape and activities that take place on it. Is there a lawn that needs to be mowed? Mowing turf close to a beehive might agitate the bees. Is there a sports field nearby? A soccer ball accidentally kicked at a beehive will definitely upset a colony. It's best to locate the garden away from lawns and larger sport areas, or have a buffer zone that may be made up of a large section of unused field or a swath of taller turfgrass that keeps errant soccer balls (and children diving for said balls) away from the beehive.

However, there are plenty of places where hives can be in close proximity to people without problems. The most important consideration is to keep the bees' flight pathway into and out of the hive clear—to keep people out of the "runway." When hives are located in a busy pedestrian area, hive managers often erect a fence. That fence does not have to be uninviting—it's just a visual cue for people to stay out.

In a residential backyard, hives can be tucked almost anywhere out of the way as long as they have sun and there's enough room for you to access the hive when it is time to harvest the honey. There are copious books on honey bee management if you're interested in learning more.

moving all your turfgrass and replacing it with a meadow, or installing bee hives.

You should also consider other people's perception of bees. While many people welcome them with open arms (figuratively, not literally, unless you are a beekeeper) and appreciate colorful gardens, others might be dubious or even frightened of them. When it comes to planting pollinator-friendly plants in a front-yard garden, think about how close the plants will be to the public sidewalk or street. For example, Anne knows that the cloud of pollinators feeding on her blue hyssop do not give two hoots about her weeding right next to them, but other people who do not know that might experience anxiety when working or walking near plants covered in busily buzzing bees. It is best to err on the safe side and not place plants that pollinators especially love (such as hyssop and mountain mint, *Pycnanthemum* spp.) immediately next to a public walkway. This protects the bees as much as the people and pets who may encounter them.

It Helps to Be Prepared

What homeowner has not gone to a garden center or nursery, seen many lovely, cheery plants, and gone a bit bananas filling up their cart? Here is how that scenario often pans out: You get all the plants home, and they all fit in the bed you have prepped—amazing. Well done, you! But as the plants begin to grow and fill in, the beds become overcrowded and the plants fail to thrive.

The problem is that most homeowners do not draw up a plan before visiting the garden center and end up with too many plants. But you will not be that person! Since you have your garden journal and this book, you know that having a to-scale drawing of your proposed space, even one roughly drawn on graph paper, allows you to develop a de-

Although we're focusing on native pollinators, we're sure there are a few beekeepers reading this book. For those folks, hives should be placed in an area with a variety of floral resources that bloom throughout the foraging season and near an adequate freshwater supply. If they're in an area where the public might encounter them, place a fence around the hives to protect both the bees and people.

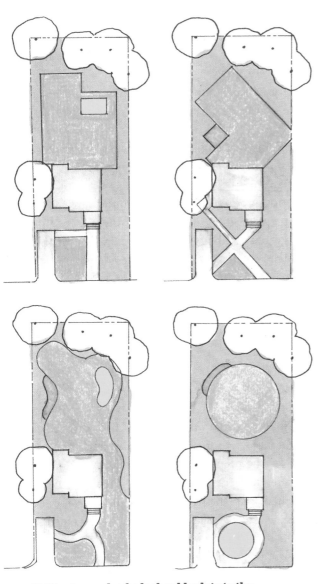

Pollinator garden beds should relate to the surrounding landscape. In the plan views above, the brightest green is turf and the darker green is existing landscape beds. Orange denotes embedded pollinator habitats, and yellow indicates stand-alone pollinator habitats.

sign with the appropriate number of plants for the space.

Drawing a Plan for Your Garden

To start, determine the shape of the bed you want. You can create a new, stand-alone garden bed or just add on to an existing garden bed, but in either case, the new garden space or expanded garden bed line should relate to existing garden spaces. Simply put, if your existing garden beds are curvilinear, then the new or extended garden bed should also be curvilinear.

If you are creating a stand-alone garden bed, make sure that the edge of the new bed is parallel or aligned with the line of the existing bed(s). The ultimate goal here is for your new bed to fit in to the existing landscape, much like a puzzle piece. When the elements of the garden, such as bed shape, are all in harmony, it makes for a more appealing garden for humans. The bees? They won't care.

Measure the area of the new bed or expanded space. If the bed is square or rectangular, excellent: simply measure the length and the width and multiply them to get the total square footage. If you have a circular garden, measure the radius (half the diameter) and use the formula πr^2 to find the area (remember, π is about 3.14). If you have an organically shaped garden, it's easiest to break it down into squares and triangles and add those areas to find the total square footage.

Then draw your garden space on graph paper. Use paper with the largest grid you can find and make one square equal one square foot. Knowing the square footage of your garden will help you determine the quantities of material—such as soil amendment, plants, and mulch—that you'll need.

Using a garden hose is a great way to explore new bed shapes, or you may use contractor's marking paint, which is available at big-box stores.

Planning Tricks and Tips

If you have trouble visualizing a new garden bed shape on paper, a great trick is to do the designing on-site first, using a garden hose to figure out the best layout. Drag the hose out and move it around to form different bed shapes and sizes. However, if your garden hose has a mind of its own (like Anne's), it might not cooperate and stay more coiled than you envision for your new garden. Pick battles you can win!

Another option is to use contractor marking paint to draw the outline of the new bed on the ground. Although marking paint is available in many colors at your local hardware or big-box store, white is best because utility companies use other colors to mark underground lines. With white paint, all site information will be clear and easy to understand, and your utility workers will thank you.

Marking paint is not cheap, and we are frugal (that way we have more money to spend on plants for our gardens). To use the paint as efficiently as possible, we dot it on the ground first, just to get a general idea of the bed line. If we don't care for the way the proposed bed line looks, we scuff out the offending dots and try again. When we're more confident that the bed lines are the way we want them, we connect the dots, making a solid outline.

Once you've decided on a shape and size for the bed, make sure you draw it on graph paper, as described above (one square for one square foot). You'll use this plan later when you select your plants.

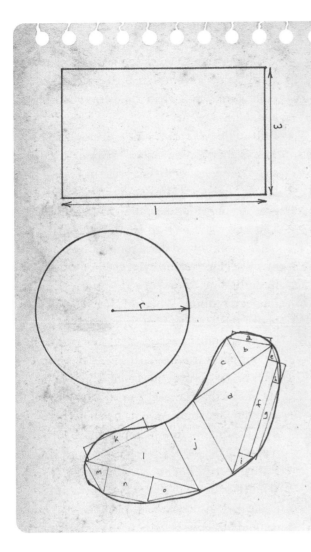

Helpful Formulas

It's important to measure the area of a planned garden beds as precisely as possible to get an accurate sense of the number of plants you'll need. Here are some formulas that are useful when you're calculating the square footage:

> Area of a rectangle or square = length x width
> Area of a circle = πr^2 (π = ~3.14; r = radius)
> Area of a right triangle = $\frac{1}{2}$ (base x height)

To determine the area of an irregular shape, divide it into squares, rectangles, and triangles, calculate the area of each, and then add the areas for the total square footage.

Tools of the Trade—So Many Plant Types!

So now that you have decided on the best location for your garden and determined the most attractive garden bed size and shape, let's move on to the plants!

A successful pollinator habitat has a mix of woody plants (evergreen and/or deciduous), herbaceous perennials, and ornamental grasses. Of course, you will want to include pollen and nectar sources for the visiting pollinators in your habitat. If there is not much plant diversity outside your yard, you might consider including plants that materials for making nests as well. These can include the leaves of plants you do not mind being cut, such as roses or azaleas, hollow stems or other crevices for nesting (rose plants are also good for this, as are grasses), or areas of bare ground, which make good nest sites.

Woody Plants
Woody plants, such as trees and shrubs, retain their branching structure year-round. They can either retain their leaves year-round (evergreen) or lose their leaves in the fall and winter (deciduous). While bees and butterflies forage for nectar and pollen on a broad variety of flowering perennials and annuals, trees and shrubs can support pollinators too. Some trees such as red maple (*Acer rubrum*) flower before most perennials, providing sustenance when bees first emerge. Our favorite woody plants that are ideal for a pollinator garden, or even as a single specimen tree or showy shrub for your yard, include the following:

* **Ninebark**: This lovely flowering shrub is native to eastern North America, but the straight species can grow too large for most yards. Select a compact cultivar, and the pollinators will flock to it in both the spring and fall.

* **Buttonbush** (*Cephalanthus occidentalis*): This is another one that can grow quite large, so be size conscious when selecting a variety. 'Sugar Shack' is a more compact version growing only four feet tall by four feet wide. The white, golf ball–size flower clusters appear in early summer and are commonly covered in many nectar-seeking bees, beetles, wasps, and butterflies for weeks on end.

* **Eastern redbud**: When this tree blooms, it's one of the harbingers of spring. In fact, even before the official arrival of spring, redbuds set our backyards and roadsides ablaze with their bright-pink-to-purple blooms. Redbuds are one of the first plants to offer pollinators an abundant source of pollen and nectar in the spring, so they're important to early pollinators.

* **Fringe tree** (*Chionanthus virginicus*): While this tree has always played twelfth fiddle to dogwood, saucer magnolia, and other common trees in our southern yards, it may be a better choice than these in some cases, and it's certainly worth considering as an addition to your landscape. It is tougher than dogwood and more dependable than saucer magnolia, and the prolific drooping clusters of fragrant, white blossoms are pollinator magnets. And as an added bonus, the summer fruits (electric-blue drupes) are devoured by birds.

Woody plants are a great addition to any garden. We especially love this ninebark ('Diablo').

Herbaceous Perennials (Forbs)

These plants go dormant in the winter but return each year (as long as the gardening gods and goddesses see fit). Historically they have not been considered structural enough to carry a garden through winter, but this is simply not true. If you plant plenty perennials that retain their seed pods and/or plant form throughout the winter (like ornamental grasses), you will have winter structure. The key here is to use a lot of perennials that have

visual interest in the winter to carry the garden through.

We tend to focus on perennial plants more than any other when we talk pollinator habitats because they provide so much nectar and pollen throughout the season for the bees, and so much color for us.

Grasses

Although they don't produce nectar or pollen, ornamental grasses are important for pollinator habitats because they provide cover for some bee species and are some of the lowest-management plants we know. They also provide stunning winter interest in a garden because, although the foliage goes dormant and turns straw-colored or tan, the form of the plant stays intact. They also add some auditory interest when the wind rustles the dry leaves.

Grasses come in all sizes and shapes, from very upright to slightly arching to weeping, and from just one foot tall to over eight. Most are perennial, but some species are annual.

Annuals

Annuals live out their life in a single year and must be replanted each year. Here in the Southeast we have two kinds of annuals: those planted for summer interest (such as some verbena and lantana) and those planted for winter interest (such as pansies). Since the Southeast spans so many USDA hardiness zones, plants that are annuals here in North Carolina might be perennials in the Deep South.

One research study found that annuals have a lower pollen content than perennials, but they may fill in seasonal gaps as well as literal gaps in your garden, and while we are not huge fans of annuals,

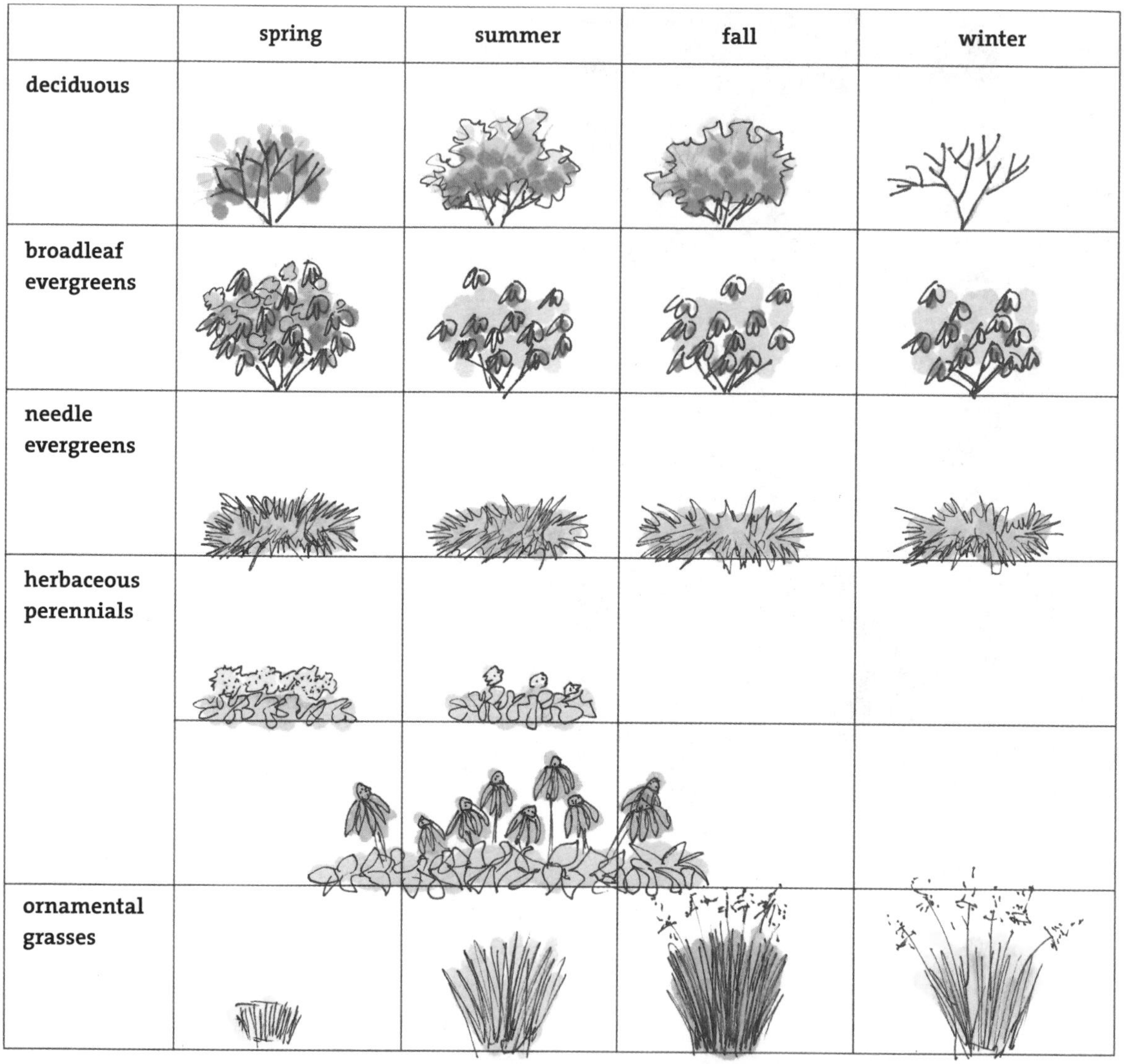

	spring	summer	fall	winter
deciduous				
broadleaf evergreens				
needle evergreens				
herbaceous perennials				
ornamental grasses				

This chart shows what different kinds of plants typically look like in each season. (The herbaceous perennials, you'll notice, often disappear entirely in fall and winter.) It's important to keep seasonality in mind when designing a garden to ensure that there's always some visual interest—and forage for pollinators.

we do like to use them when waiting for larger perennials to fill in. Too much bare ground invites weeds, and annuals can form a beautiful mass planting. Many homeowners love annuals for the pop of color they provide.

Vines

Vines are climbing plants that can be annual, perennial, or evergreen. They also have a place in a pollinator garden, especially when space is tight, as most require very little space. You might want to plant a vine as ground cover and let it sprawl, but if you want it to grow upward, you will need to provide a structure to support it. Some vines twine their main stem or trunk of the vine around the structure; some, like passionflower, twine tendrils around it; and some, such as English ivy or climbing hydrangea, just attach to the structure with rootlike holdfasts. If your vine is vigorous, like the Carolina aster (*Ampelaster carolinus*) or the passionflower vine, you will need an extra-sturdy support, such as an arbor or pergola made of wood or metal.

Variety Is Key

So you can see that gardens (of any kind, not just pollinator gardens) benefit from a variety of plant types. An all-evergreen garden will seem visually heavy and will not have as much seasonal change as most homeowners desire. A garden of all deciduous shrubs will have an awfully thin appearance come winter. Perennials can help carry a garden through the winter if chosen and massed well.

Now that you understand the tools of the trade, let's look at how to use these plant types in a garden design.

Beauty Alone Isn't Enough

A garden should, of course, be gorgeous. And it will be, by default, if it's designed well—but what does "designed well" mean, exactly? Beauty is really the bare minimum for a garden. A garden that is beautiful but lacks function or doesn't fulfill a purpose is not well designed. In this day and age, a new garden should be functional as well as beautiful; it should, for example create a habitat, mitigate storm water issues, reduce ambient temperatures, and/or provide screening and privacy—whatever is needed. The end result, if it's well designed, will be beautiful. A landscape that is beautiful but not functional is a wasted opportunity.

Research has shown that humans like the look of nature—when they are *in* nature. When it comes to their own yards, most people prefer some degree of order, neatness/tidiness, and look of deliberateness. Although most people will say they prefer a low-maintenance landscape, they have no issues with mowing a lawn once a week or shearing shrubbery. So a garden that looks cared for is important. This does not mean, however, that you can't have a meadow or wild perennial border (as long as your HOA allows it). It just means that you need to make sure that wildness has a neat, tidy edge, so there is the appearance of containment.

Don't get us wrong—your pollinator garden should be beautiful. But since beauty is in the eye of the beholder, as it were, you need to think first about what *you* find beautiful. Let's start big and work down to the details.

Planting Design Boot Camp

Now we get to the really interesting part: combining plants in a garden bed. You may be thinking, *Doesn't putting plants together take some special knowledge and training?* Well, that certainly helps. But consider this: When you got dressed this morning, how did you decide what to wear? What was your thought process in pairing that shirt and those pants? Did you repeat a color? A texture or fabric? Did you eliminate pairings because the textures were too different or the colors clashed? Did you opt to pair complementary colors together? As long as you deliberately thought about how to put together your ensemble, you were designing! You thought about design qualities, such as line, form, color, and texture, and considered major design principles, such as repetition and variety. The same thought process is used in planting design. See that? You were thinking like a designer, and you didn't even know it.

There are several approaches to designing with plants. The one favored by professionals is designing abstractly, specifying desired plant characteristics first and then finding plants that exhibit those qualities. This method ensures successful composition because it requires thinking through the combinations very carefully—what plant heights and habits (a fancier word for "form") combine well, whether you want high contrast or subtle changes in foliage textures, and how you'll incorporate a variety of flower forms, color combinations, bloom times, and seasonal interest. However, this can be an odd way of thinking for some. Plant lovers may want to jump right in and say, "I want to include this plant and that plant," which means leaving a

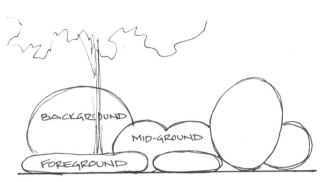

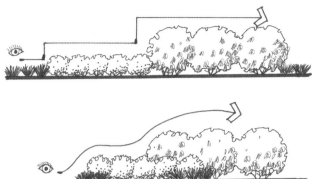

It's important to sketch elevation views in addition to bird's-eye-view plans. These elevations show visually engaging layered masses: layers for depth at left, and smooth transitions between plant layers with overlapping ends of masses above bottom; above top shows harsh transitions between masses.

lot to chance because they're not considering all the variables.

Retrieve the garden bed plan you drew on graph paper; we will start with this bird's-eye view first. Sketch circles of various sizes to represent the plants: put in larger individual plants first, then groupings of medium-size plants, and finally, masses of fillers, usually perennials and ground cover. (If you're working with an existing bed, make sure you include the plants that are already there.) The masses may vary in size and shape, from large to small, and may also include narrow, skinny masses. It's funny, but when we put pencil to paper, even though we intend to draw informal, natural-looking masses, our brain, which likes order and patterns, overrules that intention, and the first set of masses that we draw are usually uniform in size and shape. We actually have to work harder to design something looser. Be aware of this tendency if you are starting from scratch; you'll want to intentionally vary the size and shape of your plant masses. While little research has been done on this topic, it is likely that planting masses of one plant species is likely more efficient for specialist bees when they are out foraging.

Next, start constructing elevation views that look at the garden from the side for each season, just to see what the composition of heights and proportions will look like. At this point you might also add some architectural plant forms—plants with visually arresting shapes, such as yucca (*Yucca filamentosa*) or irises (*Iris* spp.). Both of these genera have dramatic, dagger-like foliage. Just try to design in general terms, not with specific plants.

At this early stage you're just trying to create a visually engaging garden. You're striving for the eye to move up and down as it takes in the composition, pausing to rest every so often on one plant. You're also exploring depth—do you have room to create foreground, midground, and background plantings? Just drawing quick, sketchy circles at this point can be helpful to at least determine plant size and shape characteristics: For example, one

These perennial
plants are especially
pollinator friendly.

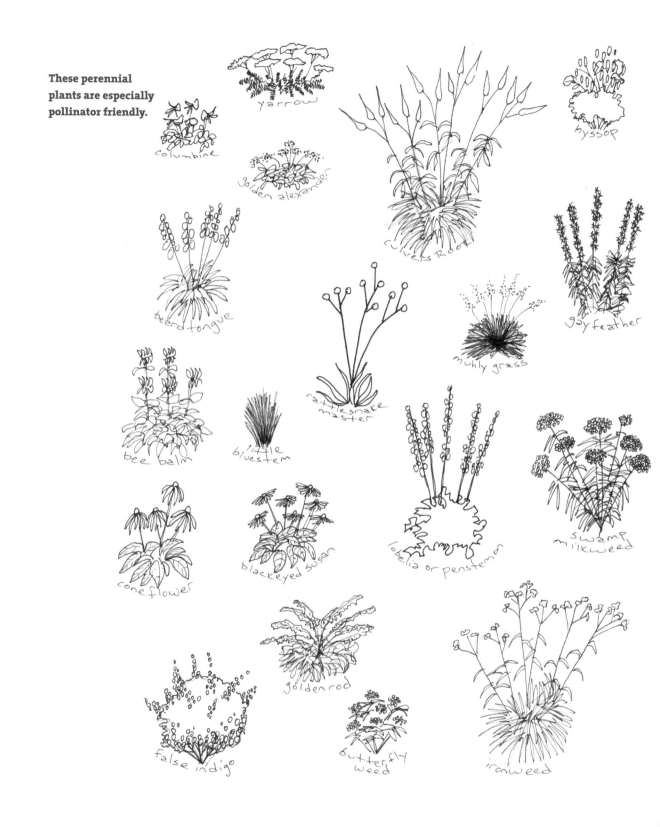

columbine

yarrow

golden alexander

culvers root

hyssop

beard tongue

rattlesnake master

muhly grass

gay feather

bee balm

b little bluestem

lobelia or penstemon

swamp milkweed

coneflower

blackeyed susan

goldenrod

false indigo

butterfly weed

ironweed

plant might be very dense and evergreen, but another might be quite open and see-through. These characteristics would make a difference where they might end up in your design. The evergreen might be more appropriate in the back of the bed to serve as a backdrop; the more open plant could be moved closer to the front of the bed as it can be seen through.

With the general sketch in hand, you can start to get more specific in thinking about what you want the plants and beds to look like. Let's start with the vocabulary we use when discussing art elements (in this case, plants!). We describe plants in terms of their design qualities: line, form, color, and texture. We then organize these design qualities using the design principles of repetition, variety, and balance to achieve a cohesive, well-thought-out garden.

Line and Form

Line is a compelling part of any design. In a garden, line can be seen in the form of a sinuous bed edge, a curvy walkway, or the outline of a plant or group of plants. Line is riveting—our eyes cannot help but follow whatever lines they see.

"Form" refers to the shape of an object—perhaps the vertical, architectural leaves of a yucca, or the gracefully pendulous branches of a weeping redbud. Closely tied to form is size. How tall will the plant grow? How long will it take to get that tall? If it's a tree, how high up does the canopy start? Can a person walk underneath it?

Revisit the plants and masses you have already sketched in and think about their form and line. It is a bit easier if you start with larger plants.

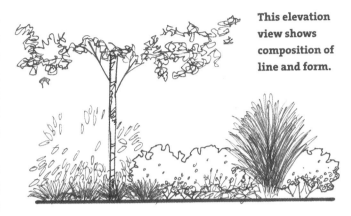

This elevation view shows composition of line and form.

Color

Color is the biggest attention-grabber in the garden. We approach color in garden design in two ways, depending on the plant type. For woody plants, the color of the foliage is the most important feature. Why foliage color and not flower color, you ask? We are interested in what is on the plant the longest period of time. Most woody plants do not flower for very long, usually just ten to fourteen days. (Of course, there are exceptions in both directions: there is a cherry tree that blooms for a single day, and then the crape myrtle blooms all summer.) For most of the year, the foliage is what you see on the plant, so we use that as our main basis for design. Flowers, while still important, take a back seat, as do fruiting characteristics.

Perennials, on the other hand, are primarily planted for their flowers. Some bloom for a long time; some bloom for a very short time. In this case it doesn't matter—the flowers are still what matter most. In addition to exploring flower color, we need to consider bloom time and flower form.

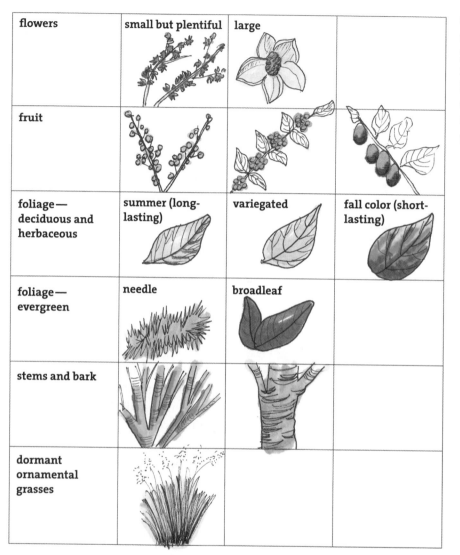

flowers	small but plentiful	large	
fruit			
foliage — deciduous and herbaceous	summer (long-lasting)	variegated	fall color (short-lasting)
foliage — evergreen	needle	broadleaf	
stems and bark			
dormant ornamental grasses			

Garden color comes from many sources, not just flowers. Since some flowers don't last very long, consider other sources of color for a continual show in your garden.

Bees love color and high contrast. Humans do as well! You've probably heard that red, orange, and yellow are considered "hot" colors, which means they have high visual energy and get our attention immediately. Blues and purples are considered "cool" colors and have a lower visual energy—they often feel more relaxed. Green is fairly neutral. So here is where color gets really interesting. If you took these general trends at face value, you might think that you could not use red, orange, or yellow

The bright pink flowers of the eastern redbud are a welcome sight in late winter and early spring. This early bloomer provides much-needed forage for native bees and honey bees this time of year, when it's one of the few plants that's an abundant source of pollen and nectar. In the fall, redbud leaves often color up a pretty yellow, for added interest.

in a garden meant for relaxation, or that you could not use blue in a high-energy garden for children. This is a very narrow interpretation of design.

Think about the last time you went to the paint aisle of a big-box store (or an actual paint store) and stood paralyzed before your range of options. You likely went in to pick up a can of pink paint, but then you saw that there are hundreds of shades of pink. It can be overwhelming! So when considering color in your garden, you can pick a color, any color—you can find shades of that color from the barely pigmented to the fully saturated and in-

tense. You can, in fact, have a high-energy, happy blue, or a more relaxed orange in the apricot and peach shades.

When it comes to pairing colors, with current trends, it would be hard to come up with a bad color combination. When we were in college, back in the day, there was a research study that showed the least favored color combination was hot pink with a vivid orange, but we see that combination all the time now. Everything is fair game. The strongest, most powerful color combinations are complementary colors—those opposite each other on the color wheel. Ever wonder why that is? It's because when the brain sees one color, it automatically looks for its complement.

However, you should consider the overall impact of your color choices and their intensity. You may certainly pair two intense complementary colors, but both of those flowers will be screaming for your attention: "Look at me!" "No, look at me!" It's like two movie stars playing the leads in a movie and demanding all the viewer's attention. There's nothing inherently wrong with that approach, but it's akin to typing in all caps. Another approach is to have one really intense color and mute its complement. For example, with a yellow-and-purple combination, you might have a vibrant yellow with a lavender shade.

Its gray-green foliage and sizable flower heads make rattlesnake master stand out in any garden. The flowers slowly dry and become yellow-brown later in the fall and into the winter, while the sturdy stalks remain well into winter, providing interest in the landscape. Despite its white flowers, rattlesnake master is still beloved by honey bees and native bees alike.

The gray foliage of mountain mint bracts is a palate cleanser with hot flower colors close by.

Since there is really no such thing as a bad color combination science-wise, we won't explore the myriad color themes in detail. But we can say that the only color theme not particularly conducive for a pollinator garden is monochromatic—using shades of just one color. Since bees generally prefer contrast, a garden that has just one color would not be as impactful. There are also some plant exceptions (because nature doesn't read science textbooks). Two plants that bees absolutely adore but that are not at all colorful are mountain mint and rattlesnake master. Mountain mint is not terribly showy, with its gray foliage and small white flowers. Despite this, there will be a multitude of pollinators all over the plant when it is blooming during the summer. The flowers of rattlesnake master are perfect globes of tiny white flowers and are also quite popular with bees.

Some people might not find mountain mint a particularly visually arresting plant, but consider

(opposite)
Create color combinations you will love in your garden: monochromatic (variations on one color, top left); analogous (colors next to one another on the color wheel, top right); complementary (colors across from one another on the color wheel, bottom right). At bottom left is another example of analogous colors with the orange flowers of the butterfly weed and the yellow leaf margins of the yucca.

The purple of the cranesbill and yellow of the golden Alexander are complementary colors.

(opposite) Combinations of different colors, textures, and shapes can add interest to your garden. Clockwise from top left: A variety of flower forms with balloon flower and orange coneflower; a combination of clusters of small butterfly weed flowers and the larger flowers of a phlox; the seed pods of a false indigo; the multicolored flowers of a phlox.

this: its gray (dare we say silver?) leaves are a wonderful foil for more colorful plants. Mountain mint gives the eyes a place to rest for a moment before they move on to take in more color. It can also be used as a buffer between colors if you feel that one is necessary.

Texture

Texture is the final design quality and the trickiest to understand. With gardens, it refers to *visual* texture, not the tactile kind. A fine-textured plant is one that has small flowers, thin stems, and small or narrow leaves. Leaf pairings are often close together, with short internodes (the space between leaf pairings). A coarse-textured plant has the opposite: large leaves and flowers, sometimes quite a bit of space between leaf pairings, and often thicker stems.

While visual texture might not seem riveting, it can be! There are two schools of thought on how to design with texture. The first approach is striving for a subtle gradation between textures: arranging plants in a way that gradually shifts from one texture to another, such as fine to medium to medium-coarse to coarse. This ends up being easy on the eye, and the plants may blend together well. The alternate approach is going high contrast: deliberately pairing a plant that is fine textured with a plant that is coarse. The juxtaposition makes the viewer sit up and really notice the two plants. Our brain's response is, "Whoa! What's going on here?!" The sum of the pairing is greater than the parts because the contrast makes plants more noticeable. Either approach is fine—which you choose just depends on what your design goals are.

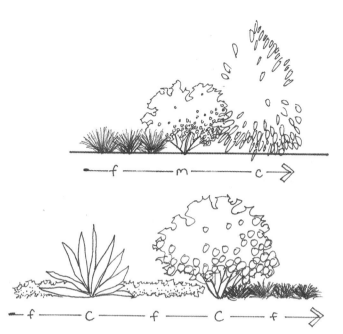

These sketches show two ways to vary texture. At top, there's a subtle gradation from fine to medium to coarse; at bottom, there's high contrast, with fine and coarse plants side by side.

Garden Design Principles

Okay, you're armed with all you ever wanted to know about design qualities. Now you get to use that "fashion sense" we mentioned earlier when we talked about why you chose to pair that shirt with those pants. (For those of you still in your pj's at four in the afternoon, we get it. Just use your imagination.)

We use design principles as strategies for organizing the design qualities of line, form, color, and texture. The ultimate goal is to create a cohesive, well-thought-out, and deliberate garden design. It is at this stage that we ask our designer brains questions like, "Should I repeat that color? How about if I create high texture contrast here? How many kinds of flowers should I include?"

There are six main principles of planting design, but the two critical ones when it comes to pollinator habitat are variety and repetition.

This sketch shows how texture, form, and habit can be varied in a garden and suggests some plants for each combination.

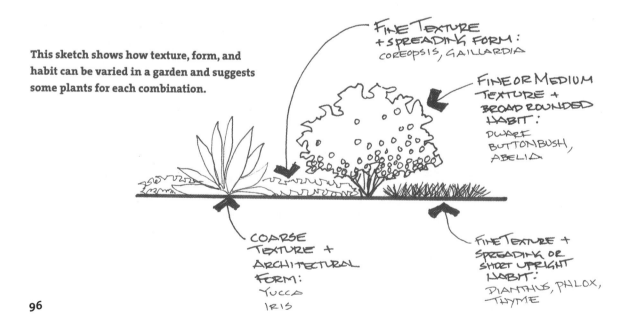

FINE TEXTURE + SPREADING FORM: COREOPSIS, GAILLARDIA

FINE OR MEDIUM TEXTURE + BROAD ROUNDED HABIT: DWARF BUTTONBUSH, ABELIA

COARSE TEXTURE + ARCHITECTURAL FORM: YUCCA IRIS

FINE TEXTURE + SPREADING OR SHORT UPRIGHT HABIT: DIANTHUS, PHLOX, THYME

"Variety" refers to having enough "stuff" in your garden to make it visually interesting at any given time. This is a little tricky because how much variety is enough is determined by (a) how the garden is experienced, and (b) your gut reaction or first inclination. To address the first point, a garden designed for sitting in often has more variety—lots of plants and other elements to hold the viewer's attention. On the other hand, a garden that will be seen primarily by people zipping by in a car usually has less variety—fewer species and larger masses. Anything more detailed is wasted on the (human) viewer. This is one of the reasons why you see hundreds of plants in just a few species planted along interstates. How much can a person take in while going seventy-five . . . oops, we mean sixty-five miles per hour?

Knowing just how much variety to incorporate also comes from the gut. Part of this, not surprisingly, is personal preference. Some people like a busy, chaotic look; some prefer a more streamlined, minimalistic look. The context should give you some clues—, the surrounding architecture, style and layout of the existing garden, and, if you're working with clients, their preferences. It also comes down to your own personal style. How much variety appeals to you? Do you like having lots of different things or prefer seeing just a handful? Either is fine—it is your personal preference.

The second indispensable design principle is repetition—repeating a design quality to help the garden appear deliberate and constructed, with the end result being a very cohesive creation. Remember, when we look at a composition (or anything, really), our brains scan it to try to make sense of it: *Do I recognize this? Have I seen this before?* Repeti-

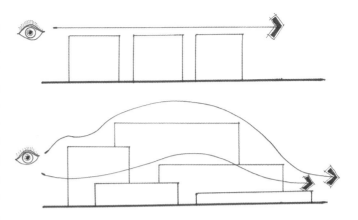

Simple, unlayered composition encourages the eye to quickly glide by (top); varied height and depth of planting encourages the eye to move around and explore.

tion of a color, a texture, a plant, or a flower form—even if subtle—helps our brains recognize the pattern, and the design becomes cohesive.

What if planting space is exceptionally tight? How do you work in enough repetition and variety? Let's say you have a narrow bed along the front of a house, under a row of windows. The bottom of the windows are four feet off the ground. The planting space between the house and sidewalk is only four feet. You don't have much room for layers, so the challenge is this: How do you make a collection of similar-size plants interesting? If we were in our classrooms, we'd wait patiently for students to raise their hands and offer up some solutions. Since we are not with you in your living rooms (or wherever you are reading this), we'll just give you some options. Since height stays essentially the same, you can and should change up other design qualities—color, texture, and/or form.

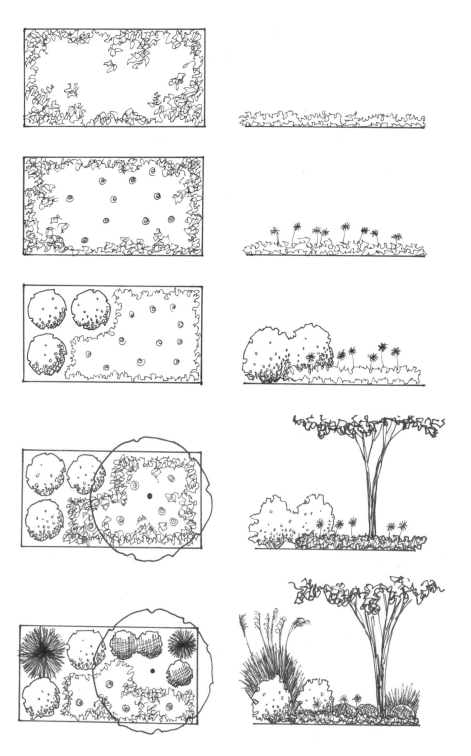

Plan views (left column) and elevation views (right column) illustrate increasing variety. The top drawings show low diversity, which builds to medium and then high diversity at the bottom.

All these are "correct" designs—any could work depending on the context and the goals of the composition. Pollinator habitats, however, need high plant diversity, so the last plan would support our bee friends the best.

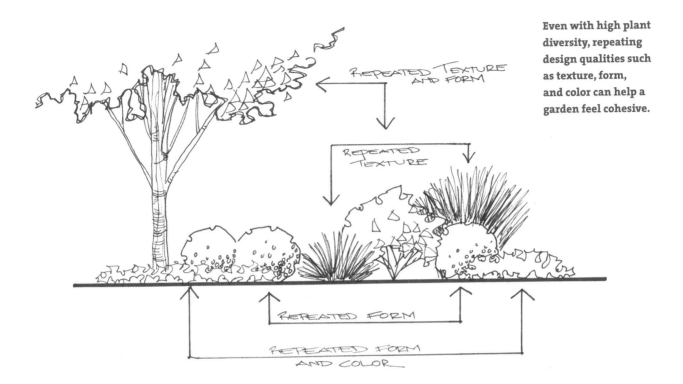

Even with high plant diversity, repeating design qualities such as texture, form, and color can help a garden feel cohesive.

REPEATED TEXTURE AND FORM

REPEATED TEXTURE

REPEATED FORM

REPEATED FORM AND COLOR

When the plants are the same height, to keep the design interesting, incorporate different textures and colors.

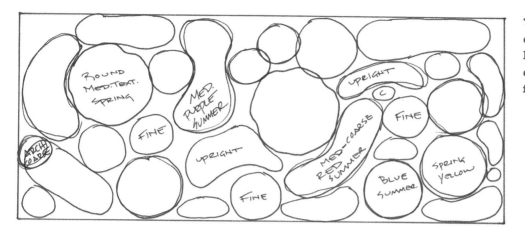

This conceptual design shows a rough layout of design qualities—texture, form, and color.

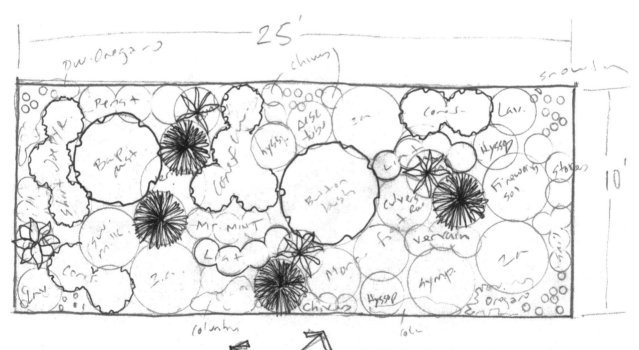

As the planting plan takes shape, some plant species are defined and some specific plants are drawn in. It probably hasn't escaped your attention that this is not a beautiful drawing. There is no need for fancy graphics here while your garden design is in progress.

Selecting Design Qualities for Your Garden

If you're starting with a clean slate, no existing plants, identify the design qualities (line, form, color, and texture) you want first, starting with specimens (plants that occur singly, as focal points) and larger plants first. On your sketch, note the desired plant size and habit, foliage color, foliage texture, and flower color. Make a note about desired bloom time as well. That way you'll be ready in the event of a tie—if two plants meet your design quality parameters and both are excellent, you can use whichever shrub provides flowers at a time of the year when the others don't. Once you've set out the desired characteristics of the large plants, then you can tackle the medium-size stuff, then the filler.

If you are starting with one or a few existing plants, note their design qualities first, then start your proposed pollinator plantings, adding larger plants, medium-size plants, and filler around them.

Now, here's where we could state a bunch of gardening rules, but we have to confess that we are rule breakers. For any given rule, we can find at least five different ways to break that rule and still have a beautiful garden. You can do this too. (Disclaimer: We are not going to bail any of you out of jail. We are talking about gardening rules only.) For example, many design sources strongly suggest that short plants always go in the front of a garden bed and taller ones always go in the back. Hogwash! There is nothing wrong with putting a tall, loose plant in the forefront of the garden, or a short, early-spring-blooming plant in the middle of a bed to put on its show before the big stuff gets going.

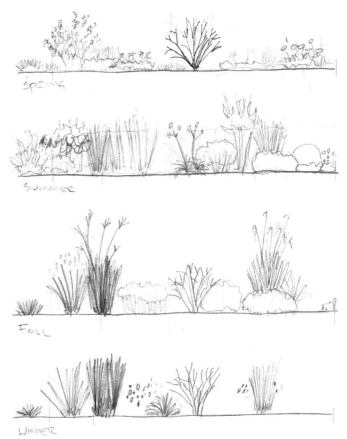

It is helpful to switch between a plan view and an elevation view like these to envision what the garden will look like in person. Note that there's a different elevation view for each season.

A Garden for All Seasons

Any garden should look attractive throughout the year, and this is especially true in the case of pollinator gardens. A garden composed of flowering perennials will look smashing from spring through early autumn but will be sorely lacking come winter. To ensure a four-season garden, you'll have to incorporate different plant types—namely, something to carry the garden through the winter months, something that still communicates, "Hey! There's a garden here!" Additionally, late summer / early fall is the hardest time for pollinators as pollen and nectar sources become less prevalent in the heat and dryness of August and September. Think carefully about how to incorporate more late-blooming plants in your garden—it will pay off in the long run.

The seasonal charts in the next section will help tremendously in this effort. As you start to choose specific plants, create your own chart off to the side of your garden drawing. The true benefit of a seasonal chart is twofold. First, it helps you to factor in seasonality while you are designing. When Anne is working on a planting design, she makes charts as she goes. It might be a handwritten or hand-drawn chart that she keeps on the side of her desk, or it might be a digital chart. As she works her way through the design, she makes sure there are no seasonal gaps. In this way, the seasonal chart is used as a design tool. Second, if you are working with a client, the chart is also a communication tool: by looking at the chart, the clients will be able to quickly and easily understand how their future garden will have interest year-round.

Keep in mind that different species of the same genus may flower at different times. This information is often noted in plant catalogs and plant labels with the words "early blooming," "midseason blooming," or "late blooming." When you include multiple species in a pollinator habitat, pollen and nectar offerings are greatly increased because the

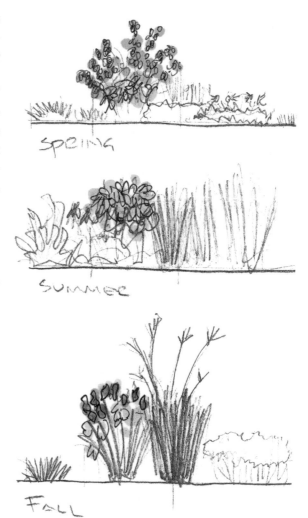

SPRING

SUMMER

FALL

It can be tricky to think of what a garden will look like throughout the seasons—especially when plant catalogs only focus on bloom time. So draw it out! In this drawing, we've zoomed in on the indigo. This is a plant that has gorgeous flowers in the spring. When the flowers are finished, the foliage persists and is a lovely light green. Later on, some baptisia species will have lovely seed pods.

Anne loves to design smaller gardens by hand (as opposed to using computer graphics). As she selects her plants, she makes a rough list off to the side of her desk and makes seasonal notations to make sure she's designing for all seasons. In this respect, this list becomes a design tool because it helps her amend her plant selection along the way. Are there too many gaps in the spring column? Now is the time to revise the list, before the plan is finalized. If Anne is designing for a client, the final plan will be drawn beautifully and the plant list and seasonal chart will be done on the computer.

Don't Neglect Seasonality Charts

A seasonality chart can help you ensure you have all the seasons covered in your garden. If you wait to create your chart until after finalizing your design, you will inevitably discover gaps and will have to rework your design. If you are a professional designer, a seasonality chart is also a powerful communication tool when presenting to clients and stakeholders. Lists and schedules that note flowering times are helpful, but our brains do infinitely better in picturing the garden as a whole throughout the year when that information is shown graphically.

flowering time has increased. For example, some species of false indigo (*Baptisia* spp.) bloom in late spring while others bloom in early summer.

Also consider what a plant looks like when it finishes blooming. Many perennials develop lovely seed heads (like coneflowers) or seed pods (like false indigo), which many people find attractive. If you (or your client) does not like the look of the seed pods, simply tuck the false indigo among other plants that are taller than it.

This chapter has been quite a journey so far, but you have done all the really hard work by carefully selecting your site, defining the size and shape of your garden, arranging plant masses, determining the design qualities you prefer, and figuring out

SAMPLE GARDEN PLANT LIST WITH FULL RANGE OF SEASONALITY

		Seasonal Interest			
Scientific Name	Common Name	Spring	Summer	Fall	Winter
Aquilegia canadensis	Eastern red columbine	■			
Asclepias tuberosa	Butterfly weed		■		
Baptisia 'Purple Smoke'	Indigo	■		■	
Callicarpa americana	American beautyberry			■	
Camellia sasanqua	Camellia	■		■	■
Cercis canadensis 'Rising Sun'	Redbud	■			
Coreopsis lanceolata	Lanceleaf tickseed		■		
Echinacea purpurea	Purple coneflower		■	■	
Eryngium yuccifolium	Rattlesnake master		■	■	
Fothergilla 'Mount Airy'	Dwarf fothergilla	■		■	
Geranium 'Rozanne'	Hardy geranium		■	■	
Hylotelephium 'Autumn Joy'	Autumn joy sedum		■	■	
Ilex glabra	Inkberry	■	■	■	■
Liatris pycnostachya	Prairie blazing star		■	■	
Lonicera sempervirens	Trumpet honeysuckle	■	■	■	■
Monarda fistulosa	Bee balm		■		
Nepeta racemosa 'Walker's Low'	Catmint		■	■	
Penstemon smallii	Small's beardtongue	■			
Pyncnanthemum incanum	Mountain mint		■		
Rhus aromatica	Fragrant sumac			■	
Salvia rosmarinus	Rosemary	■		■	■
Rudbeckia hirta	Black-eyed Susan		■	■	

		Seasonal Interest			
Scientific Name	Common Name	Spring	Summer	Fall	Winter
Schizachyrium scoparium 'The Blues'	Little bluestem		■	■	■
Stokesia laevis 'Peachie's Pick'	Stokes' aster		■		
Symphyotrichum oblongifolium 'October Skies'	Aromatic aster			■	
Tulbaghia violacea	Society garlic	■			
Yucca filamentosa	Adam's needle	■	■	■	■
Zizia aurea	Golden Alexander	■			

■ flowers ■ foliage ■ fruit ■ seedpods ■ seed heads

how to arrange those qualities in your garden according to design principles. You're now ready for the big finale: plant selection!

Plant Selection

If you don't set your design parameters first, plant selection can be the toughest part of any garden design: if you know plants well or just love them, it can be hard to narrow your list of wants, and if you don't know plants, the staggering number of options can be daunting. Designing your garden the way we've suggested, by sketching out the context and design qualities you desire, is incredibly helpful because it serves as a filter—you are now looking for plants with specific design attributes. Also, setting out to design a pollinator garden is another great way to limit your plant choices, because you already know you want to include the best plants for pollinators. That will reduce your list of plant options from hundreds to a much smaller number.

Selecting the right plants can also be tricky because few sources have all the information you need. Catalogs, websites, and plant labels give you sun and shade requirements, USDA hardiness zone, and average size at maturity. But that often does not tell the whole story, and sometimes the information is misleading or wrong. Let's break this down a bit.

The USDA Plant Hardiness Zone Map charts the average low temperatures across the United States and Canada. Zone 1 starts up in Canada with the average minimum temperature bracket of –15°F to –10°F. The warmest zone is 11 (45°F to 50°F), in Hawaii and the Florida Keys. Here in

SEASONALITY CHART FOR WOODY PLANTS

Scientific Name	Common Name	Plant Type	Size
Abelia spp.	Abelia	E, S	3′–6′ tall × 3′–6′ wide
Acer rubrum	Red maple	D, T	40′–60′ tall
Callicarpa americana	American beautyberry	D, S	6′ tall × 6′ wide
Ceanothus americanus	New Jersey tea	D, S	3′–4′ tall × 3′–5′ wide
Cephalanthus occidentalis	Buttonbush	D, S	5′–10′ tall × 4′–8′ wide
Cercis canadensis	Eastern redbud	D, T	15′–20′ tall × 20′–25′ wide
Chionanthus virginicus	White fringetree, grancy greybeard	D, T	12′–20′ tall × 12′–20′ wide
Clethra alnifolia	Clethra, sweet pepperbush	D, S	4′–8′ tall × 4′–6′ wide
Fothergilla gardenii	Dwarf fothergilla	D, S	3′ tall × 3′ wide
Lindera benzoin	Spicebush	D, S	6′–12′ tall × 6′–12′ wide
Oxydendrum arboreum	Sourwood	D, T	20′–30′ tall × 20′ wide
Physocarpus opulifolius	Ninebark	D, S	5′–10′ tall × 6′–10′ wide
Rhus aromatica	Fragrant sumac	D, S	2′–6′ tall × 6′–10′ wide
Vaccinium corymbosum	Highbush blueberry	D, S	6′–12′ tall × 6′–8′ wide

Plant Type: E = evergreen, D = deciduous, T = tree, S = shrub

the Southeast, we're mostly in zones 6 through 10. Florida alone goes from zone 8, in the Panhandle, to zone 11, in the Keys.

Even places in the same zone don't necessarily have the same climate, however. A website or plant catalog may say a plant is hardy to zone 7—but zone 7 in California is not at all the same as zone 7 in North Carolina. What makes the two coasts different? If you are thinking about water, you are exactly right—it's precipitation and humidity. So

the hardiness zone is not the be-all, end-all characteristic. It is just one piece of the puzzle. Different soil types also play a major role. The red clay of the Southeast has its fair share of challenges.

Plant labels and descriptions also do not tell you if a plant is invasive. This information might also change from area to area depending on site conditions (for example, a plant that's not invasive in dry soils might be invasive in saturated soils). Although the regional information presented in this book is

Origin	Spring	Summer	Fall	Winter	Notes
Exotic					
Native					Early bloomer
Native					
Native					
Native					
Native					
Native					Summer fruit loved by birds
Native					
Native					
Native					
Native					
Native					
Native					
Native					

■ flowers ■ foliage ■ fruit

excellent, should you find yourself needing more, or should your site have unique pollinator habitat needs, we strongly suggest contacting your local cooperative extension agent.

The tables below list some of our favorite pollinator-friendly plants. We only use well-behaved, non-bossy plants that are adapted for the Southeast. The tables include scientific name, common name, size and habit, and a key to general seasonality.

Once you have selected all your plants, you can rest easy knowing that you are practically ensured a successful composition because you have thought through every decision carefully. Well done, you! Your garden will be the talk of the neighborhood.

If you have drawn your plan and plants to scale, you can count up all the individual plants and make your shopping list. For masses of ground cover and perennials, use the table below to calculate plant quantities based on total square footage.

PERENNIALS AND ORNAMENTAL GRASSES

Scientific Name	Common Name	Plant Type	Size
Agastache spp.	Hyssop	Perennial	12"–30" tall × 12"–30" wide
Aquilegia canadensis	Eastern red columbine	Perennial	2' tall × 1' wide
Asclepias incarnata	Swamp milkweed	Perennial	3'–4' tall × 3'–4' wide
Asclepias tuberosa	Butterfly weed	Perennial	2'–3' tall × 2' wide
Baptisia spp.	Indigos	Perennial	3'–4' tall × 4' wide
Bouteloua gracilis 'Blonde Ambition'	Blue grama	Grass	1'–2' tall × 1'–2' wide
Coreopsis spp.	Coreopsis, tickseed	Perennial	1'–2' tall × 2' wide
Cuphea micropetala	Mexican cigar plant	Perennial	3' tall × 3'–4' wide
Echinacea purpurea	Purple coneflower	Perennial	2'–3' tall × 2'–3' wide
Eryngium yuccifolium	Rattlesnake master	Perennial	3'–4' tall × 2' wide
Eutrochium spp. / *Eupatorium* spp.	Joe-pye weeds	Perennial	3'–6' tall × 3'–6' wide
Gaillardia spp.	Blanketflower	Perennial	2'–3' tall × 2'–3' wide
Geranium spp.	Hardy geranium	Perennial	6"–12" tall × 18" wide
Knifophia spp.	Red hot poker	Perennial	3'–4' tall × 3'–4' wide
Liatris spp.	Blazing star	Perennial	2'–4' tall × 1'–2' wide
Lobelia spp.	Lobelia	Perennial	2'–4' tall × 2'–4' wide
Monarda spp.	Bee balm, horsemint	Perennial	2'–4' tall × 2'–4' wide
Nepeta racemosa 'Walker's Low'	Walker's Low catmint	Perennial	1'–2' tall × 1'–2' wide
Panicum virgatum	Switchgrass	Grass	3'–7' tall × 3'–7' wide
Penstemon smallii	Small's beardtongue	Perennial	18"–24" tall × 18"–24" wide
Pyncnanthemum spp.	Mountain mint	Perennial	3'–4' tall × 3'–4' wide
Rudbeckia spp.	Black-eyed Susan	Perennial	2'–3' tall × 2'–3' wide

■ bloom time (for pollen and nectar)　　■ foliage used for habitat (cover, nesting)

Origin	Spring	Summer	Fall	Winter	Notes
Exotic		●			
Native	●				Reseeds readily, not a nuisance
Native		●			Better in wetter sites
Native		●			Better in drier sites
Native and nativars	●				
Nativar		●	●	●	Native to western North America but not the Southeast
Native and exotic		●			
Exotic		●			
Native		●	●		
Native		●			
Native		●	●		
Native		●			
Exotic	●	●			
Exotic		●			
Native		●			
Native		●			
Native		●			
Exotic		●	●		
Native		●	●	●	
Native	●	●			
Native		●	●		
Native		●			

PERENNIALS AND ORNAMENTAL GRASSES *(Continued)*

Scientific Name	Common Name	Plant Type	Size
Salvia spp.	Salvia	Perennial	2′–5′ tall × 2′–5′ wide
Schizachyrium scoparium	Little bluestem	Grass	1′–2′ tall × 1′ wide
Sedum spectabile 'Autumn Joy' (recently renamed to *Hylotelephium* 'Autumn Joy')	Autumn joy sedum	Perennial	1′–2′ tall × 1′ wide
Stokesia laevis 'Peachie's Pick'	Stokes' aster	Perennial	24″ tall × 18″ wide
Symphyotrichum spp.	Asters	Perennial	2′–4′ tall × 3′–5′ wide
Symphytum spp.	Comfrey	Perennial	1′–2′ tall × 1′ wide
Veronica spp.	Speedwell	Perennial	1′ tall × 1′ wide
Veronicastrum virginicum	Culver's root	Perennial	4′–6′ tall × 4′ wide
Vernonia noveboracensis	Ironweed	Perennial	5′–8′ tall × 5′ wide
Zizia aurea	Golden Alexander	Perennial	18″ tall × 24″–36″ wide

■ bloom time (for pollen and nectar)　　■ foliage used for habitat (cover, nesting)

Origin	Spring	Summer	Fall	Winter	Notes
Native and exotic		■			Long bloomers
Native		■	■	■	
Exotic			■		
Nativar	■	■			
Native			■		
Exotic		■	■		
Hybrid		■			
Native		■			
Native		■			
Native	■				Can be bossy

Got Weeds? Good!

We would be remiss if we didn't address the American lawn. It is hard to have a perfect, lush yard in the Southeast without using a lot of resources. So consider not weeding! Some of the ubiquitous plant species that often pop up in lawns include excellent pollinator plants, such as white clover and dandelion. They are green, provide nectar and/or pollen (and dandelions provide pollen and nectar early in the season, when bees first emerge), and have attractive flowers.

In this chapter, we tackled design concepts, pollinator garden design, and plant selection. You might already be outside with marking paint laying out a garden bed or at a garden center buying (more) plants! The next chapter will explain how to install your new pollinator habitat.

Yards that are exclusively grass are not ideal for bee pollinators. Many plants that are considered weeds are very rich in pollen and nectar, making them important forage for bees. This yard sports a healthy population of dandelions; other common "weeds" that are good for bees include all types of clover, chickweed, and violets.

5

Digging in

Installation and Management

You have developed a plan for a pollinator habitat. Now you need to figure out how to implement it. There are many decisions to be made. Which direction you go depends on how much you want to dig in the dirt, how patient you are, and how you want to allocate your resources.

Before You Start

Many states require that prior to digging deeper than sixteen inches on your property (even for landscaping), you must call the Joint Utility Locator to come out and mark any underground utility lines, such as phone, cable, water, gas, and electric lines. (Dial 811 before you dig!) This is a legal requirement that was put in place to protect homeowners. It is also a free service, and who doesn't like free stuff? While you don't have to call until you're ready to dig, we like to call during the design phase so we know where all the lines are ahead of time and can add them to our site analysis notes. This saves us from designing an elaborate planting bed on top of an important and fairly shallow utility line. We call again to have the lines re-marked when we are ready for installation.

Be advised that when the various companies come out to mark, the lines they make are just a guide. The utility line might not be exactly where they marked. For example, the line may be located within two and a half feet on either side of the marked line, for a total window of five feet. That means if you dig within that five-foot span and you hit a line, you're liable and must pay to fix the line. If you hit a line that falls outside of that window, it is the company's fault, and they should come out and fix it at their expense. What is most important,

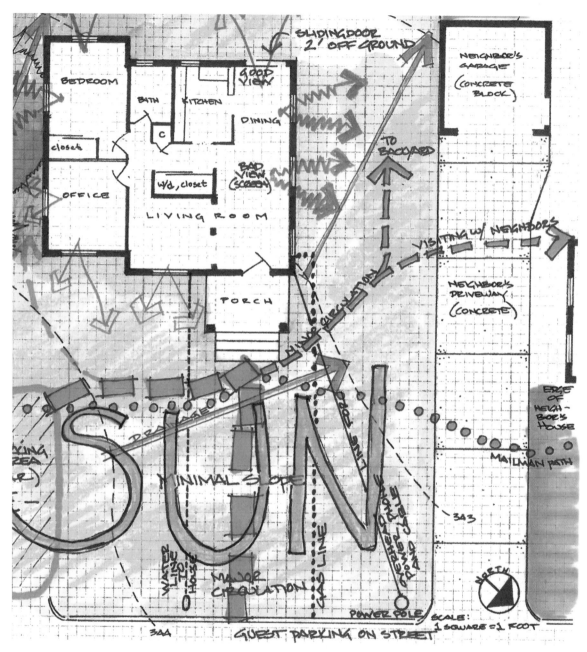

This site analysis of a yard notes footpaths, good and bad views, sun exposure, slopes, drainage, and, importantly, utility lines, both underground and overhead.

A new construction site with the topsoil removed and subsoil that's been compacted by machinery. These are not ideal planting conditions!

however, is safety. You can dig within the five-foot zone, but just be careful. We highly suggest hand-digging rather than using machinery within the five-foot window. The depth of utility lines varies depending on many factors and can change because of the final grading of a newly constructed site or erosion, so never assume that an underground utility is at a specific depth.

A cut cable or phone line may be a simple inconvenience, but a damaged electrical, water, or sewer line is much more complicated and time-consuming to fix. A damaged gas line is extremely dangerous and should be avoided at all costs. Calling 811 at least week before you dig will help you to avoid injury, expense, and the inconvenience of going without services.

Garden Bed Preparation

Wouldn't it be nice to start with a clean slate? A beautiful grass- and weed-free garden bed with crisply defined edges and dark, easy-to-dig-in, fluffy soil, eagerly awaiting new plants. We don't know where you can find that kind of space naturally, but if you do, let us know and we will move there immediately. For now, we'll focus on how you can create that kind of bed yourself.

We do not want to get too much into the weeds here (no pun intended!), but we would be remiss if we did not recommend getting a soil test report from your local cooperative extension office or state soil-testing lab. All you have to do is submit a soil sample, and they can tell you what nutrients you need to add and how to adjust the pH if necessary. A quick internet search will tell you what options are available in your state, as well as how to take a soil sample, how to submit it, and how to read the report once the results are in. No matter what your results say, though, the good news is that a pollinator garden can be built in any kind of soil conditions, provided the soil is well draining, has appropriate levels of macronutrients and micronutrients, and has a pH around 6.5.

Very few gardeners, however, start out with perfect soil. The best approach is to work with the soil you have and make a few modifications, such as adding compost. New Orleans chef Emeril Lagasse used to say that cream cheese is the duct tape of cooking because if you make a mistake, you can just add cream cheese to solve almost any problem in tasty fashion. Compost is the cream cheese

This is an existing landscape that might be a candidate for renovation. The evergreen shrubs are too large and need to be routinely trimmed so they don't block the windows. The homeowners could consider removing those and replacing them with a smaller species that does not require pruning. While they're at it, some of the turf could be removed and replaced with a pollinator garden. Just sayin'.

of gardening. We'll talk more about the benefits of compost in the following pages.

Typically, when working with homeowners, we encounter one of two scenarios: (1) newly constructed home sites where only subsoil remains after grading and compacting a parcel of land; or (2) garden renovations for established properties that have existing plants and very different soils. Each situation requires a different approach to garden installation. Of the two, new construction is more difficult in terms of the amount of work that needs to be done to re-create healthy soil. Garden renovation is tricky in terms of removing existing grass and/or weeds.

New Construction

A newly constructed site has unique landscape challenges. It is a clean slate only in that there is ample opportunity for new plantings. There likely needs to be quite a lot of work done to prepare the soil for long-term plant growth and health. In most instances a builder or developer has removed the existing topsoil to do the necessary subsoil grading and compaction to support structures. Ideally, the topsoil—which contains all the organic matter, including nutrients and important soil microbes plants need to grow and thrive—should be replaced after construction is completed, but usually this is not practical. This means that the first task at any new-construction garden site is to add organic matter back into the soil.

The easiest way to do this is to add compost. You can purchase it in bags from a garden supply store if you have smaller garden spaces, or, if you're creating a larger garden, you can pick up or have delivered a truckload of compost. Over the long term, you can make your own compost with landscape materials (such leaves and grass clippings), and for extra bonus points, you can compost your food scraps in a worm bin to create vermicompost. For more information on vermicomposting, Rhonda Sherman, extension specialist at North Carolina State University, has published many helpful fact sheets (available through the North Carolina State Cooperative Extension website) about setting up your own worm bin at home. It is easy to turn household food scraps and yard trimmings into nutritious soil amendments, which, when added to garden soil, promote plant growth and reduce attacks by plant diseases and pests.

Compost benefits the soil in several ways. First, it adds pore space, which increases space for oxygen and creates a path for water to infiltrate the soil. Second, compost adds nutrients back to the upper soil layer, re-creating the top two soil layers (referred to as "the O and the A horizons"). Last, compost adds microbes and other microorganisms that help break down nutrients, making them available for uptake by plants.

Research has shown that adding compost to a whole prepared bed is more beneficial than adding compost to each individual planting hole because the plant roots will quickly grow out past the edges of the planting hole and spread into the surrounding soil. So when preparing your new planting bed, amend the whole bed to accommodate and encourage that root growth. You might not plant everything all at once, but when you're ready to add more plants, the bed will be ready and waiting.

Garden Renovation

In a garden renovation, a common project is expanding an existing bed to accommodate new plantings—in this case, pollinator plants. This requires removing turf or weed cover, and or removing ornamental plantings no longer wanted. Here is a conundrum you might have experienced during a garden renovation project: soil disturbance (e.g., removing existing grass and/or weeds and tilling to work up a garden bed) invites opportunistic plants and exposes weed seeds that have lain dormant in the darkness to daylight, causing them to

spring to life. Some homeowners use chemicals to kill off these weeds prior to planting, but there are effective nonchemical options that are safer for the environment.

Solarizing and sheet mulching are no-till, nonchemical options for killing weeds, but they need to be started up to several months before planting, depending on what time of year you start and what weeds you are trying to kill. Solarizing is securing a tarp over the area where you want vegetation and weeds killed. Cut the plants down as low as possible first, then secure a tarp over the area. The sun beating down on the tarp and the reduced moisture together kill off most plant growth underneath. This works faster in the summer and can take longer during winter months.

Sheet mulching is when you cut down existing growth and then layer newspaper and/or cardboard and organic matter (mulch, manure, compost) over the area you want to prepare. The layers will block any light from getting through to the weed layer, as well as provide a physical barrier that smothers the existing weeds. Keeping the layers wet by spraying them with water will aid in their decomposition as well as encourage worms and microorganisms to the area. This method takes about six months, so it is best to start in the fall with an eye to the spring planting season.

Plant-Buying Options

Considering Size When Buying Plants

Regardless of your role in the creation of a pollinator habitat—be it landscape contractor, community volunteer, or homeowner doing the work yourself—likely you will not be buying mature plants for installation. However, a planting plan will show perennials and shrubs at their full size and trees three-fourths of mature size to make sure plant quantities are correctly calculated without over- or underplanting, as we discussed earlier. For homeowners who hire a design professional to design their garden, this can often cause confusion when they see the planted garden because the plants installed are quite a bit smaller than they were on the plan showing mature plants. It is the responsibility of the landscape designer and/or contractor to manage expectations and explain the installation process.

Plant nurseries sell plants in a variety of sizes and stages of maturity, and in a variety of ways. Which size you should buy depends on several factors, including how soon you want the garden to have a substantial impact, the growth rate of any given plant, and, of course, your project budget. The end result will be disappointing and anticlimactic if you stretch your budget as far as possible by purchasing only small plants. It still costs a pretty penny, but the reaction after planting everything is often, "Where did all my money go?" Bigger plants have a bigger impact.

But purchasing all larger sizes also has its drawbacks. The most obvious being that, because larger plants cost quite a bit more and require more labor to install, you might be able to install only a portion of the garden at first. Larger plants also take more time to establish and have to be nursed along for several years, most notably with regular irrigation. That flies in the face of most homeowners' desire for low-management and low-input landscapes.

Something else to consider when selecting plant sizes is the growth rate of your plants. It does not make sense to buy a large fast-growing plant, such as butterfly bush, when a sprig will grow large in just one season. Unless you are preparing a landscape for a special event and you need a showstopping plant, buying a five-gallon or even three-gallon fast-growing plant is, frankly, unnecessary. The other side of that equation also holds true. For slow-growing plants, such as Japanese maple (*Acer palmatum*; not a tree known for supporting pollinators but a notoriously slow grower), it makes sense to put more money into buying a larger plant. Sure, you can find one-gallon Japanese maples, but they will not amount to anything eye-catching in your lifetime, unless you are currently a three-year-old with superior reading skills.

Therefore, a smart strategy for both creating an impactful newly installed landscape and staying on budget is to mix plant sizes, with some small, some medium, and maybe a few large.

Plants are available for installation in several forms, each with its own pros and cons. In the next few sections we will lay out what you need to know about using containerized plants and growing plants from seed. We infinitely prefer these forms to balled-and-burlapped plants, mainly for ease of installation and adaptability to its home in a new garden, and because of budget restrictions, so these plants are not included in this discussion.

Buying Containerized Plants

Containerized plants are plants sold in, you guessed it, containers. They are available in a wide range of sizes. Small plants are most commonly sold in flats of thirty to fifty plants per tray. It is not uncommon in the fall to see pansies in large flats at the local farmers market, or six-packs of small, four-inch pots of fall annuals or summer vegetables. The next size up is quarts, then gallons. The larger you go, the older the plant is and the more developed the roots and shoots are.

Depending on the impact you are looking for and numbers of plants you are planting, it may be best to grab a flat of inexpensive annuals for the border of your garden or to plant around the mailbox, a few quart-size plants such as herbs, and one or two gallon-size plants as your impact plants.

The benefit of installing larger plants is that they have an immediate visual impact. The downsides are that the larger the plants you buy, the greater the cost, and larger trees and shrubs require more care after planting because they have a disproportionate root-ball-to-canopy ratio. Keep in mind that once planted, the root ball that was in the container has to support the plant growth above the soil. The more disproportionate they are in size, the harder it is for that plant to get established in its new garden spot. When selecting containerized plants, it is best to start with medium-size plants; that way you have room to adjust. If you are over budget, you can buy some smaller plants. If you are under budget, you can buy some larger plants.

It is important to remember that newly installed plants will have open space between and around them until they fill in. They will eventually touch each other, as a landscape plan created by a professional shows, but it will take some time for them to grow that large. In between the new plantings is prime real estate for weeds to not-so-magically appear. This is an excellent place to plant annuals, which will fill the space, outcompete most weeds, and provide a burst of color for the landscape. You

Plants come in a variety of sizes. Pictured from left to right: 4 inch, 1 quart, 1 gallon, 3 gallon, and 7 gallon.

can also opt to plant perennials or ground cover in these spaces, with the understanding that the perennials might have to be removed (or possibly moved to another area of the garden) as the other plants mature. Mulch is also an option for preventing weeds, but remember that the more mulch you use, the fewer nesting opportunities you are providing for your ground-nesting bees.

Direct Sowing

Another method growing in popularity is directly sowing your pollinator habitat with seeds. Usually plants are started from seed in a greenhouse or a sunny space in your kitchen, and then a wee plant is transplanted to the garden. But you can also sow pollinator-friendly seeds directly into a garden bed or an area that you don't want to spend a great deal of money on, such as areas along your sidewalk, walkways at church, or sloped areas. You can even "guerilla garden" around your neighborhood, periodically tossing out handfuls of wildflower seeds. (There may or may not be some wonderful cosmos popping up around a certain neighborhood in southwest Raleigh that supports an abundant and thriving bee community.)

The most obvious benefit of direct sowing is the cost. Seeds are much less expensive than established plants. Direct sowing can also be much less time-consuming in the long run. It does, however, require irrigation, as once the seeds start to germinate, they cannot dry out. If you plan on direct sowing a large area, then it is most cost effective to purchase seed in bulk. We prefer this option because you can customize the seed mix. We often buy a pollinator seed mix appropriate for the Southeast and then add extra quantities of a particularly favored species or two to the pre-mixed seed. For example, a seed mix listed as "Southeast friendly" may include around fifteen or so different pollinator-friendly species, with a healthy blend of annuals and perennials, and maybe a few grasses thrown in for those cavity-nesting bees to nest in in the fall. This mix may not include your favorite pollinator-friendly species, but this is not a problem: simply add an extra order of milkweed or coreopsis to ensure that your area will buzz and hum with colorful, dancing pollinators all season long.

Direct sowing also requires more patience—while that's fortunately still free, it's difficult for some of us to come by. One downside to direct sowing a perennial garden is that it takes longer for blooms to emerge. A direct-sown perennial garden will not look especially robust in the first year. A lot

Share and Share Alike

Sharing plants among friends and family is a meaningful and inexpensive way to add plants to your garden. Why buy native columbine when it reseeds so readily? Ask a friend who has some if they'd care to share.

of vegetative growth will come up, some of which will flower, but for the most part, it will not be a glorious meadow. This is easily remedied by sowing a mix of perennials and annuals. The annuals will provide flowers during the first year, and the perennial flowers will emerge the following season, or the following year.

Plant Sources

Make sure you buy containerized plants and seeds from reputable sources that can guarantee that neonicotinoids (those insecticides that are so dangerous for bees) were not used while growing the plants prior to selling. These chemicals are taken up by plants and can remain in all parts of the plant, including pollen and nectar, for a long time, including the seeds. It can be tricky to make sure your plants weren't treated with neonicotinoids because there are no regulations requiring plants that have been to be labeled. Even if the retailer does not use neonicotinoids, the wholesaler or initial grower might have. Therefore, always ask before buying, and try to stick with suppliers who grow their own stock. Buy seeds labeled "organic" from reputable suppliers.

Additionally, make sure you buy only healthy, vigorous plants that adhere to the *American Standard for Nursery Stock*. That is to say, plants should be healthy, well-formed, and free of pests, including weeds, which may try hitching a ride in the container. In the case of a professional installation, a landscape professional should inspect the plant material before purchase or delivery to ensure the best material available is taken to the job site.

Proper Planting Times

Unlike in other parts of the United States, where winters are long, gray, and often so cold that when you go outside and sniffle your nostrils stick together, you can plant just about year-round here in the South. As long as the ground isn't frozen, you are pretty much good to go. If you can handle the heat and humidity of the summer, you could sneak in some planting then as well. So gardening year-round is possible in the Southeast. However, just because you *can* (meaning, you can get a shovel into the ground), doesn't mean you *should*. Anne might find a plant she's been hankering for in the middle of summer and buy it, but she knows that once it's planted, she will have to check on it at least once a day, maybe more if there hasn't been any rain. She is happy to do that in her own garden, but she would never require that kind of management from a client.

Landscape professionals agree that the best times for planting are spring and fall. The key in spring is finding that sweet spot after the last frost but as far in front of the hot summer months as possible. Sometimes that window is pretty small. Once we are into the summer in the Southeast, any newly installed plants have to be watered regularly. You will often find the greatest selection of plants available in nurseries in the spring, because that is when most homeowners are thinking about tackling a new garden. Herbaceous materials put on root growth as well as leaves and flowers in the warm season, and many folks are itching to get out into their gardens and start planting.

Fall is another great time for planting because plants still have an opportunity to get established before the cold winter temperatures set in, fall temperatures are a little more reasonable than summer ones, and rain is likely. Fall is also the time when woody plants put on new root growth. Fall is particularly advantageous because there is less competition from weeds. However, nurseries carry a more limited selection of species in fall, and often the plants that are left have been on the lot all summer. Again, there is a sweet spot, or at least a cut-off time, for planting: perennials need at least a few good weeks to get established before the cold sets in and they stop growing. Here in North Carolina, we are comfortable planting perennials and most ornamental grasses through the middle of October. After that, it can get a bit dodgy, as cold snaps tend to pop up with little warning. Once you have decided on the best time to plant your garden, it is finally time to get to work.

On public or municipal sites (such as hotels, restaurants, and apartment complexes), there is often a discrepancy between the best horticultural

This shrub planting detail shows the size of the hole and the root ball. Note that the top of the root ball is even with the ground. Backfill should be existing soil mixed with some compost. It's better to amend an entire planting bed rather than a single planting, but often gardeners are just planting a few plants at a time.

knowledge and the need to satisfy certificate-of-occupancy requirements. Some municipalities stipulate that state planting must be completed before inspectors can sign off on the project and the owners can move in. This is bad news for plants if a project is finishing up in the summer, which, as you know, is the worst time to be planting. Because of this, some municipalities and green infrastructure groups are amending their ordinances to coordinate better with the best horticultural practices.

Planting Techniques

In the world of perfectly and ideally installed gardens, an entire garden bed would be prepared, its soil amended, and the new plants planted in one fell swoop. However, many of us are digging individual holes for a few newly bought plants and planting as we go. While this might not be the ideal situation, you can still make it work.

You may have heard the phrase "Dig a fifty-dollar hole for a five-dollar plant." We are not sure

of its origins or age, but the adage holds true today. A hole should be at least twice the width of the root ball, but no deeper than the soil line in the pot. Use the excess soil to build a small saucer around the planted root ball at the edge of the canopy or plant mass. Mulch up to the saucer, but not within it. To water the plant, turn on the hose to just a trickle and leave the hose end within the saucer. Slowly water the plant over several minutes. A quick blast will do little because most of the water will evaporate before it reaches the roots, where water is needed most.

You may pull a plant out of its container only to discover that there is little soil in there and the voluminous roots grow around and around themselves, taking up almost all the container. This is what is known as a pot-bound or root-bound plant. It has just been in the container too long. Have no fear—there is an easy fix. Take a sharp knife or other pruning tool and score down the sides of the root ball in several places, and then across the bottom. Some people even cut off the very bottom of the root ball. This looks extreme, and you might even feel bad doing it, but trust us, the plant will thank you for it: it allows the roots to grow out again. If they're not cut, they often keep growing around in circles, which reduces growth and ultimately results in the death of the plant.

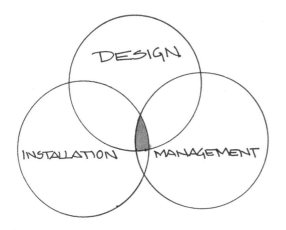

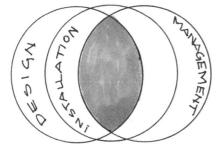

Often design, installation, and management are addressed separately. A traditional Venn diagram (top) implies that they overlap just a little. However, one impacts the rest: the design is only as good as the installation techniques and management practices used. It is more helpful to think of them as overlapping (bottom). While you are still designing, you should be thinking about installation and management. This will ensure a successful pollinator habitat for a long time.

Pollinator Habitat Management: If You Build It, They Will Come ... but Then What?

We prefer the term "management" over the traditional term "maintenance." "Maintenance" implies we're trying to keep the habitat in a singular state of being, which is not only undesirable but also unsustainable. "Management" is a more accurate reflection of our interaction with a growing, living, and ever-changing entity.

There is a strong correlation between design, installation, and management. A traditional Venn diagram would lead you to believe that there is a tiny

This landscape is low in plant diversity, making it less beneficial for pollinators.

These landscapes are rich in plant diversity. More plant diversity means more pollinator diversity.

sweet spot where these three aspects of landscape design overlap. In reality, we should strive for more overlap, with installation and management playing a larger role during the design phase. Every line drawn on a plan represents a plant that will have to be installed and managed. A bed line or garden edges will have to be mown or otherwise kept neat and orderly. It is imperative, then, that management requirements are considered early on.

Knowing the management regime up front—who will be responsible for caring for the habitat, the management schedule, and the skill level of the management team—can dictate the garden style and layout. For example, if you're creating a community or school garden that has limited management, you'd be wise to pick a planting style that is free-form and has a wide variety of plants, so that when a weed pops up, it is less noticeable.

Management Schedule

As early as late winter, homeowners and other landscape caretakers start preparing their gardens for the spring. During that first warm day in early February, we want to get outside and begin working on our gardens while soaking in some beautiful southern sunshine. We cut back old growth on shrubs, perennials, and ornamental grasses. Fresh layers of mulch are spread. As we prepare for new planting, we work up new beds, tilling the soil or just digging generously sized holes for new plants. Some people spray chemicals on their lawn, including preemergent herbicides, which are designed to prevent leafy weeds from popping up in your lawn later in the spring.

Garden management timing becomes especially important to a bee-friendly garden. Native bees overwinter in the ground or in cavities and do not emerge until temperatures reach approximately 57°F. Depending on where you live in the southeastern United States, 57°F occurs somewhere around March and April. It's best not to disturb the bees before they emerge. This means that even though you have the urge to begin cutting back the dormant growth of ornamental grasses during that warm snap in February, it is better for the bees that might be in the stems if you wait until later in the season. Alternatively, you can bundle the stems together after cutting them back and leave them in the garden until later in the season. Resist disturbing the soil or top-dressing mulch until the temperature in your area reaches 57°F.

The best thing you can do to encourage and support ground- and stem-nesting bees is to do nothing to stems and the ground aside from planting

≈ 57°

Several garden tasks that are typically done in late winter or early spring, such as cutting back ornamental grasses, spreading mulch, and planting new plants, can be disruptive to overwintering bees. Consider doing these tasks on the other side of the dotted line shown, when temperatures have warmed up to at least 57°F, when bees tend to emerge.

more plants that provide nesting and foraging opportunities for them. If you are so inclined, it is still a fine idea to cut back your perennials during the summer to encourage more and longer-lasting blooms, but as you get to the end of the summer (late July and August), discontinue this so there will be seed heads and stems in the garden during the winter months. This not only gives nesting bees a place to lay their eggs and remain safe throughout the winter but also provides seeds for songbirds and winter visual interest for humans.

In an ideal world, there would be no spraying of toxic chemicals. However, there are some instances when that is necessary. Today, especially with concerns over Zika and other mosquito-borne diseases, homeowners and municipalities alike are increasing their efforts to reduce disease vectors such as mosquitoes by spraying chemicals that kill these pest populations. Unfortunately, these pesticides also kill bees and other beneficial insects.

As a homeowner, you have some control over what you spray and when. If you must spray, it is best to do so when the bees are not foraging. Spray early in the day, before bees are out, or in the evening, after the bees have hunkered down for the night—as the labels of many of these insecticides mandate. The risk posed to bees and other beneficial insects is influenced by both how toxic the pesticide is and whether the insect is exposed to it. Spraying when bees are not out foraging helps to reduce the risk of exposure, as does selecting a chemical that dissipates and breaks down quickly in the environment.

If you are a beekeeper or very engaged bee advocate, the most important thing you can do to protect your bees from accidental exposure is communicate with your local municipal mosquito-control programs. You can learn about what products they use and when (they should also be spraying after hours and not during the day). You can be added to a "no spray" list or place signs such as the yellow-and-black-striped Bee Aware signs in your yard to denote the presence of bees.

Caring for Plants through Establishment

Although plants in nature do not require human intervention in order to survive, suburban and urban areas are not natural environments. In fact, the landscapes in which we live do not resemble native landscapes any more. Nutrient-rich topsoil has been stripped away in the construction of roads and buildings. The remaining subsoil has been compacted by machinery and is now devoid of organic matter. Drainage patterns have been altered. Soil fertility is reduced. Infiltration (how quickly water soaks back into the soil) is diminished. Temperatures are hotter because of pavement. Not so natural, eh?

Because of these changes, any new plant in a constructed landscape—native or not—needs to be taken care of through the period of establishment. Establishment is the stage during which a plant puts down roots and "gets happy" in its space. The length of establishment varies by plant type and roughly translates to one growing season for perennials, two seasons for shrubs, and three or more for trees. Of course, you will be planting in amended soil, existing soil with a few inches of added compost (remember, we discussed this at the beginning of this chapter; stick a Post-it there so you don't forget), and watering regularly in periods without rainfall.

You may have noticed that we haven't mentioned fertilizing. If you've amended with compost and you've mulched your beds, there should be plenty of nutrients in the soil and there shouldn't be a need for extra fertilizer. When in doubt, collect a soil sample from your garden and get another soil test.

These few management strategies will set your plants up for success. And successful plants mean a successful pollinator paradise, as well as happy gardeners!

Time to Play in the Dirt

So there you have it—the nitty-gritty details of installing and managing your pollinator habitat. It is hard to pick our favorite chapter in this book, but the next one is really exciting: in it, we will take you through a series of examples of how we have created pollinator habitats at different scales. You may find inspiration in one, or possibly all, of the examples we share. You will see how you can use the principles in this book to make fabulous, butterfly-watching, bee-nest-site-laden, just-sittin'-and-readin'-worthy pollinator gardens, no matter how much or how little space you have to dedicate to the cause. There is no garden too small to make a difference.

Pollinator Gardening Big & Small

Whether you have room for just a few plants or for a vast garden, any additional habitat helps improve the world for pollinators, which in turn, will sustain humans for a while longer on this planet we call home. This chapter will discuss how to incorporate pollinator habitats at a variety of sizes, from postage stamp–sized courtyards to acres of public or private land. We hope that it will excite and inspire you, and once you plant your niche, you can sit back and enjoy the fruits of your labor.

No Yard? Plant a Container Garden

Perhaps you do not have any yard at all and you are reading this book when the first harbingers of spring are beginning to emerge. You may be a bit jealous of your neighbors who are planning large compost deliveries to enrich the soil where they will plant their multitudes of nectar-rich, colorful flowers. Don't worry—you too can plant nectar-rich posies and support pollinators!

If you have a list of favorite plants that you have been pining over, now is the time to pull it out and make some difficult choices. Pick out a couple of favorites, find a large, beautiful, and sturdy pot, pull out your gardening hat, and get planting.

A well-chosen pollinator plant or three in a container can provide sustenance and protection for our pollinator friends, without the expanse or expense of a larger-scale planting. Even though it's small, a container garden can support pollinators and bring welcome color and interest to a hardscaped area such as a patio or apartment balcony. It is also an easy introduction to growing plants for the novice gardener. All you need is a container

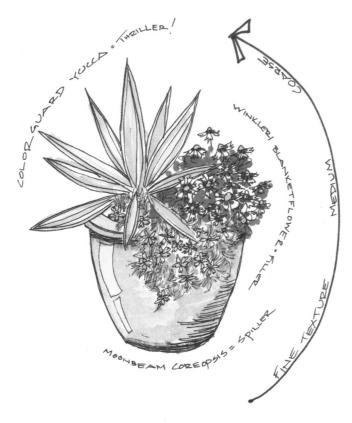

COLOR GUARD YUCCA = THRILLER!

COARSE

WINKLERI BLANKETFLOWER = FILLER

MEDIUM

FINE TEXTURE

MOONBEAM COREOPSIS = SPILLER

Even a single container planting can benefit pollinators. A well-designed container garden has a thriller, a spiller, and a filler, and includes a variety of colors, forms, and textures.

that has holes in it for drainage, some potting soil, and—the best part—some plants.

The Golden Rule of Container Planting

The golden rule of container planting states that glorious container gardens most often include a spiller, a thriller, and a filler. A spiller, unsurprisingly, is a plant that spills over the edge of the container. These plants help keep container plantings in scale. Trailing vines and flowering plants help connect the plantings to the container while hiding and softening its edges. Great selections for spillers include creeping zinnia (*Sanvitalia procumbens*),

sweet alyssum (*Alyssum maritimum*), trailing or creeping snapdragon (*Asarina procumbens*), and lantana (*Lantana camara*).

The second element in your container should be a tall plant or plants that add height and texture to your container. This is the thriller. It should be the eye-catching, architectural, upward-reaching specimen in the mix. Select these plants based on the size of your container; ideally, they would grow to be about twice as tall as the container itself. Plants that are traditionally used as thrillers in the South include ornamental grasses, yucca, and dwarf canna lilies (*Canna* spp.). You could also mix it up and add something like a tomato plant (be sure you buy one with smaller tomatoes, such as grape, cherry, or Roma tomatoes), sweet or hot peppers, or eggplants. These might be especially welcome if they are on your patio next to your grill. Want some grilled peppers to accompany your burgers? Well, look at that; you have some delicious peppers right there.

Filler plants are those that fill the rest of the space in the container, bridging the tall thrillers and trailing spillers while adding lots of interest to your arrangement. Examples of fillers include gentian sage (*Salvia patens* 'Patio Deep Blue'), giant hyssop (*Agastache rupestris*), flowering maple (*Abutilon* spp.), and Rozanne hardy geranium (*Geranium* 'Rozanne').

Remember that larger containers will not dry out as fast as smaller containers, so go as large as

This container planting has a thriller, spiller, and filler arrangement with pollinator-friendly (and other) plants. The thriller in this photo is purpletop vervain (notice the height it brings, although the thriller may just as frequently be large, leafy plants that take up more space in the arrangement or sport large striking blooms). Fillers include begonias, dianthus, and petunias (which can do double duty as spillers depending on the variety). The spillers include the lovely lime-green ornamental sweet potato, which will continue to drape along the side of the container all season long. Also spilling along the edge of this container are the daisylike blooms of the bidens.

you can for the space and as your wallet will allow, especially if you are growing vegetables in and among your flowers.

Foraging for All

Want to do double or triple duty with your container garden? Nestle some herbs in the container. Herbs such as basil, lavender, oregano, and rosemary are perfect fillers and will thrive on your deck, balcony, or front step, provided you offer them enough water and plenty of sunshine.

Some herbs, like cilantro and basil, become bitter after they bloom, although that is when they provide food for pollinators. In these cases, you may prefer to use the herb while it is growing in the spring and then, once it bolts (flowers), leave it for the bees. Alternatively, consider harvesting some plants for human consumption and let some plants flower for pollinators.

Don't want to have to pick and choose? Select herbs that will flower all season, such as chives and pineapple sage. This way, you will be providing an appealing buffet for bees and flies throughout the season, the chives will give you a surprising addition on top of Nana's classic deviled eggs (she will forgive you, we promise), and you can toss the pineapple sage leaves into a cold beverage for a unique twist on agua fresca.

The Parkway (or Devil Strip)

In urban areas, most homeowners' property does not go all the way to the city street. Often a city right-of-way extends across the road and then across the public sidewalk (if there is one) to just

a foot or so past the sidewalk. This area, known as the parkway (or "devil strip" because it's dry and far away from any water spigot), is often where underground utilities are located, and the city right-of-way is there so those lines can be accessed. If no public sidewalk exists, that space is still commandeered by the city right-of-way in case a sidewalk ever needs to be built.

The parkway is typically neglected and is often bare or covered in parched and weedy turfgrass, or maybe it's a lush stand of turf that is not used for anything but must be watered and mowed weekly during the growing season. Although you might not naturally think of it as a good gardening spot, the parkway is actually a prime area for a pollinator habitat. This often-wasted space only needs some soil amendment and careful plant selection to become a place wonderful butterflies will soon be plentiful.

There are a few important things to know before you start planting in the parkway. First, homeowners are expected to manage that area (even if it sim-

needs to do utility work directly under your pergola. This is a case when it is likely better to ask permission than forgiveness. Finally, be sure to check with your homeowner's association to make sure that you can plant in your parkway. If the city allows it but the HOA does not, you may not plant there. The stricter covenant prevails.

If you do decide to convert this small stretch of ignored turf into a patch of pollinator habitat, consider whether people park on the street where your new habitat will be located. If so, you need to consider where vehicle doors will swing open (and possibly hit your plants) and where someone may step out of the vehicle. Using short plants that allow car doors to swing over them is a wise move. Consider including an artistic element of large stepping-stones or pavers to allow a person firm footing upon exiting their vehicle. Also (do we need to say this?) we do not recommend planting brambles (*Rubus* spp.), yucca, hollies with spines (*Ilex* spp.), or creeping juniper (*Juniperus horizontalis*) here because of these thorny plants' ouch factor.

Some of our favorite plants to add to a devil strip are annual ornamental flowers that do well in small spaces and are a good source of nectar and pollen. These include zinnias (*Zinnia elegans*), salvia, celosia (*Celosia* spp.), and sunflowers. These are plants that are easy to direct sow or start indoors and then transplant outside once the weather turns nice.

ply means mowing it during the warmer months), even though they do not actually own it. Often municipalities allow small plantings in the parkway with the understanding that if the city ever has to dig there, they may tear out whatever planting is in the way. For plant-enthusiast homeowners, this is a risk worth taking. Second, it is always best to check with your municipality prior to creating anything considered semipermanent or permanent, including built elements, so that you do not run the risk of seeing your hard work destroyed if the city

Your parkway might also include a mixture of companion plants that go well together, such as tomatoes (*Solanum lycopersicum*), borage (*Borogo officinalis*), and marigolds, or squash (*Cucurbita* spp.), oregano, and sunflowers. There is no hard-and-fast rule about what must be planted here, and really, you can plant any of your favorites in this space. Allow this space to give you the opportunity to get creative. Maybe you will inspire your neighbors to plant in their devil strip too.

Pocket Gardens in Commercial and Communal Settings

Pollinator habitats can be incorporated into any sunny setting you can imagine, no matter how small. Consider adding a small garden to an outdoor area at an office, where employees can eat lunch and take breaks. If you need to justify this idea to your boss, share with her that research has shown that being out in nature helps people recover from mental fatigue and improves focus.

Many businesses and office buildings have large signs out front either on turf or among simple evergreen plantings. Sometimes they're even just on mulch. These spaces offer an opportunity to create a pocket pollinator garden. This approach has an added benefit, besides all the usual benefits of a pollinator garden: If the business sign is in turf, it has to be mown around every week in the warm seasons. Adding plantings in an easy-to-mow bed shape makes the area much easier to care for. It also draws attention to the sign.

Think about small public spaces that might be good spots for a handful of pollinator-friendly wild-

Small courtyards can be made into pollinator gardens too. Add container plantings for additional texture and effect.

flower seeds. An outdoor waiting area or bus stop, the area around a stop sign, the edge of a parking lot ... There are many small communal spaces that are rife with green space that could be converted into pocket gardens to benefit pollinators.

Health-Care Facilities

Garden spaces at health-care facilities can include pollinator-friendly plants. This is another opportunity for a win-win situation. Pollinators benefit from having more food and habitat, hospital visitors have a place to relax (and even regain their composure if need be) that offers a reprieve from the sterile hospital interior. For patients, a garden can bring welcome fresh air, warm sunlight, botanical fragrances, and sounds of nature. Custodial care facilities that utilize sensory gardens for additional counseling spaces and meditative purposes might find that pollinator-attracting plants could provide additional benefits to the users of the gardens. Patients and caregivers alike can benefit from bright and cheery pollinator-friendly plants, and the animals that visit them, in these spaces.

Interestingly, outdoor space inspired a therapist to come up with a type of therapy called eye movement desensitization and reprocessing (EMDR), which is sometimes used to alleviate the distress associated with traumatic memories. As she walked through a garden, the therapist watched a butterfly that visiting plants on one side of the garden path, then on the other, and then back again. She noticed that she felt substantially more at peace after following the butterfly's flight path with her eyes, without moving her head.

Another lovely addition that offers an opportunity for ample butterfly viewing, as well as fruit for both birds and human health, is elderberry (*Sambucus canadensis*). The plant supports pollinators, and the fruit has antiviral properties that are good for humans. You could pay thirty dollars for a small bottle of elderberry syrup at your local health food store, or you could easily make your own.

Home Is Where the Bees Are

Many neighborhoods have a homeowners association (HOA), a group of individuals elected to enforce the neighborhood appearance guidelines as established by the development owner. Historic neighborhoods might have other covenants to adhere to for appearance or historic appropriateness. While these regulations do not stipulate outright that pollinator habitats are prohibited in a front yard, they might state that front yards cannot have meadows or massed grassy plants over a certain height. These guidelines are not concerned with function, only aesthetics, and are mainly intended to maintain a standard or uniform look for the neighborhood.

It's easiest to create a pollinator garden at a residence because it is private property. Even when there is an HOA to contend with, pollinator habitats for native bees can be built into existing landscaped areas or created from scratch. Residential gardens are also easiest because there are fewer stakeholders involved than in other gardens, such as community gardens or public green spaces. The homeowners can design their habitat any way that suits them (within HOA regulations).

No matter the size or style, pollinator gardens in residential landscapes can offer a welcome respite for busy bees.

Foodscaping

While it is not a new concept, sometimes it is worth reminding traditional gardeners that a robust vegetable garden can be commingled nicely with a pollinator habitat. There are some wonderful books about this concept, which is called foodscaping (one of our favorites is *The Foodscape Revolution*), so we will not spend too much time on it here. Just remember that your garden does not need to be a formal vegetable-only or pollinator-only garden—you can design it any way you like. In fact, the beauty of foodscaping is that you can plant vegetables alongside your favorite pollinator plants, showy foliage plants, and everything in-between.

Another way to approach mixed plantings is called "companion planting," which is specifically designed to reduce pest pressure on your plants. According to the 2020 *Old Farmer's Almanac*, "Tomatoes make great neighbors for basil plants in the garden—and on the plate!" The basil helps prevent hornworms on the tomatoes, and the tomatoes provide some shade for the basil. If you have had aphids or beetle problems on your cucumbers in the past, try planting marigolds and nasturtiums among the cucumber vines to repel these and other voracious pests. Melons and squash need pollinators before they can set fruit. To invite these insect visitors into your garden, try planting dill, fennel, and parsley near your cucurbits. Planting vegetables as part of your pollinator-friendly landscape brings benefits that will last all season long, and your garden will be bountiful as well as beautiful.

137

This foodscape (belonging to our friend and notable author Brie Arthur) has vegetables, grains, and pollinator plants aplenty. Here we see larkspurs, poppies, and wheat.

Community gardens are fantastic places for pollinator gardens.

Community vegetable gardens benefit in a number of ways from having perennial pollinator plants incorporated into their landscape. The vegetables will be happy nestled among companion plants such as marigolds, sunflowers, borage, and cosmos. These pollinator-friendly plants draw in bees, which increase tomato yields; squash bees, which pollinate zucchini; and hoverflies, whose larvae will eat aphids before the aphids eat your collards.

Planting flowers and herbs with vegetables can protect your vegetables from insect pests and encourage pollinators, which makes your veggies more productive. While you're weeding your allotment at the community garden and catching up with your fellow gardeners, be sure to gather some of your sunflowers, black-eyed Susans, and celosia for your breakfast table. Take an extra bouquet to your neighbor and tell them about your bees, and maybe they will plant a container with flowers for the bees too.

Rain Gardens

Perhaps there are stormwater issues on your property. Do you feel that you should put in a rainwater garden (a beautiful recessed garden designed to capture runoff) at the expense of a pollinator paradise? You don't have to choose. In your new rain garden, plant species that grow well in the sunny, humid South and are also pollinator friendly, such as bee balm, cardinal flower, blazing star (also known as "gayfeather," *Liatris* spp.), and asters. Need a tall architectural element in your garden? Choose sweet Joe-pye weed (*Eutrochium purpureum*) or ironweed (*Vernonia* sp.), which will draw in butterflies and bees alike. Any garden can serve several functions as well as provide beauty.

Rain gardens can be pollinator gardens too. When a garden or design element has more than one purpose, we call it "stacking functions."

Schools and College Campuses

Pollinator habitats can be worked in anywhere. In educational settings they not only improve the appearance of grounds but also offer additional teaching opportunities. In grade schools and middle schools, science teachers can take advantage of a garden by taking the lessons outdoors and teaching young kids about the environment and their place in the world. A garden also provides an opportunity to discuss where their food comes from (hint: it's not the grocery store).

At colleges and universities, visible pollinator habitats can also provide teachable moments. They can help raise environmental awareness through signage and garden activities and/or tours, and professors can use them to teach students in any major about the relationships among plants, an-

Schoolkids love getting their hands dirty, especially in a garden. Learning firsthand about plants and pollinators can instill a lifelong love of science and art.

imals, and humans. We often utilize pollinator gardens to teach our students about how solving environmental problems requires pulling expertise from multiple disciplines. If we need information on vermicompost, we bring in a compost and vermicompost expert. If we are establishing a rain garden, we invite the folks in the Department of Biological and Agricultural Engineering to give a talk to the class. Much like pollinators and the flowers they visit, experts and students alike benefit from these interactions as ideas are cross-pollinated from teacher to student and student to teacher.

On our campus at North Carolina State University, we use pollinator habitats for graduate and undergraduate research projects, and even for educating the greater bee-aware community. For one of our recent projects, we installed a pollinator habitat at a local arboretum and gave tours, held field days, and hosted volunteer groups who were interested in our Citizen Science project educating the public about pollinators. This was a wonderful opportunity to bring community members, students, and retired faculty together to learn about native and nonnative pollinators, how to identify them, and how to strategically select plants to support pollinators. While we were teaching all these interested folks about bees and beetles, we were also able to share information on how landscape management decisions affect the environment and pollinators. No garden is too small to use as a pol-

A rooftop pollinator garden at Talley Student Center, North Carolina State University

A small sliver of turf that had to be mowed weekly was transformed into a beautiful garden that requires less management. Plants are labeled in a way that is easy for people running or biking past to read.

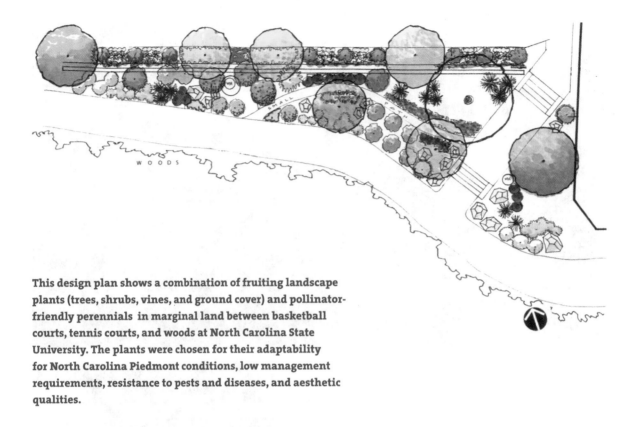

This design plan shows a combination of fruiting landscape plants (trees, shrubs, vines, and ground cover) and pollinator-friendly perennials in marginal land between basketball courts, tennis courts, and woods at North Carolina State University. The plants were chosen for their adaptability for North Carolina Piedmont conditions, low management requirements, resistance to pests and diseases, and aesthetic qualities.

linator habitat, and no opportunity is too small to use as a teachable moment.

If you're adding plantings on a college or university campus—whether on a university campus or where campus space transitions to a residential neighborhood, such as a planting corridor along a streetscape—be sure the plantings fit in with the university's strategic plan. Here at North Carolina State, for example, there is an overall framework plan for spatial connections, paths, and activity areas, and a general suggestion for permanent plantings along the main edges of campus. Polli-nator habitats can certainly be a part of this land-scape, but they must fit within those parameters. Perhaps pollinator gardens on campus can help bridge the campus and surrounding community by making campus green space an amenity for the entire community. Residents of neighborhoods abutting a campus might choose to take evening or weekend strolls through the garden. Not only can creating pollinator gardens promote using campus green spaces as amenities, but it could also be a way to showcase research being conducted at the university.

Greenways and Bike Trails

Marginal areas that are often turf and have to be mowed once a week—such as the areas along bike trails, greenways, fencerows, and the edges of sport fields—are excellent places to create pollinator habitats. Converting at least some of these areas to pollinator habitats would give them more aesthetic appeal, and once they're established, they would require less management by the grounds crew—and, of course, they'd benefit pollinators.

The Garden as Art: A Museum Setting

In 2016 the North Carolina State University Gregg Museum of Art and Design moved into the former chancellor's residence in Raleigh. The museum's director, Roger Manley, wanted to make the sunken formal garden in the rear more modern and environmentally friendly. "Could this be a pollinator garden?" he asked the design team. That directive set in motion an incredible design-build experience for students enrolled in the school's planting design course.

This pollinator garden is unique in that it is functional in terms of providing food, cover, and nesting for pollinators, but it is also, most decidedly art. The design had to respond to the retained historic layout of the overall garden (brick wall edges, original planting bed lines, turf center); but it also had to respond to this new function as a place of art and to the modern new wing of the building. Students researched the site and possible plants, developed multiple design ideas, and merged those

A newly installed pollinator garden at the Gregg Museum of Art & Design, North Carolina State University

ideas into one final plan. After presentations and layers of campus approval, students planted the garden.

Botanical Gardens and Arboretums

Botanical gardens and arboretums are excellent places to incorporate pollinator habitats—they have a lot of visitors to educate about pollinator and habitat issues. The Lady Bird Johnson Wildflower Center at the University of Texas at Austin,

The pollinator garden at the Gregg Museum of Art & Design includes black-eyed Susans, bee balm, and grama grass (left); and anise hyssop, grama grass, spent Joe-pye weed, white coneflowers, and veronica (below).

for example, highlights native plants from across the state. With 284 acres of gardens, woodlands, and savannas, it displays more than 970 species of Texas native plants on-site. This botanical garden is a model for beautiful, sustainable landscapes and hosts about 185,783 guests annually.

Need some inspiration before you begin designing your perfect pollinator paradise? Pull out your school-spirit throw blanket, pack a picnic basket, and grab a friend. No matter where you live in the historic South, there is probably a botanical garden or three close enough for a day trip.

The list below is by no means exhaustive, but it is an excellent sampling of botanical gardens and arboretums that have noteworthy pollinator habitats and educational programs:

Crosby Arboretum, Picayune, Mississippi
JC Raulston Arboretum, Raleigh,
    North Carolina
Lady Bird Johnson Wildflower Center,
    Austin, Texas
New Orleans Botanical Garden, New Orleans,
    Louisiana
Norfolk Botanical Garden, Norfolk, Virginia
North Carolina Botanical Garden, Chapel Hill,
    North Carolina
Sarah P. Duke Gardens, Durham,
    North Carolina
State Arboretum of Virginia, Boyce, Virginia
Waterfront Botanical Gardens, Louisville,
    Kentucky

Golf Courses

When you think of golf course landscapes in the southeastern United States, what comes to mind? Most likely pine trees and azaleas, and you would not be wrong. Many of the most famous golf courses in the South are replete with manicured turfgrass, bright pink azaleas, and towering longleaf pines. However, these areas, spanning anywhere from about 70 acres to over 200, offer perfect opportunities for wildlife habitats.

We have worked with golf course superintendents all over the Southeast and Southwest. One of the most widely publicized projects was our work at the Pinehurst Resort in Pinehurst, North Carolina. In 2010 Bob Farren, director of golf course maintenance there, undertook a historic project by removing over fifty acres of Bermuda grass and restoring the natural beauty of the native Sandhills ecology. Now, nestled among the sandy bunkers are blue Sandhill lupine (*Lupinus diffusus*), broadleaf pink purslane (*Portulaca amilis*), and pineweed (*Hypericum gentianoides*). Hole number 4 was planted with a pollinator-friendly seed mix, and on sunny afternoons in the summer, you can spot Indian blanket (*Gaillardia pulchella*) covered in shiny sweat bees and partridge pea (*Chamaecrista fasciculata*), which has extra floral nectaries to attract nectar-loving bees, butterflies, and ants. Basil bergamot (*Monarda clinopodia*), which loves this environment, is a favorite of bumblebees and native bees.

On golf courses Pinehurst No. 2 (top) and No. 4 (bottom) at the historic Pinehurst Resort, Bermuda grass was removed and replaced with many native plants, including a number of pollinator-friendly ones.

Be Bold, Be Brave, Be a Pollinator Champion

While this chapter has probably given you a great deal of ideas and, hopefully inspiration, it may also have given you a sense that the plantings you were thinking of might not be enough. That smart-looking galvanized-metal washtub you found at the flea market and planted with red geraniums (for the hummingbirds), bright green mint (for your tea), celosia, and sweet alyssum (the spiller!) is beautiful on your porch steps, but it might seem awfully small in the scope of the greater world and all the threats facing bees.

Do not fret. Remember, any habitat is a good habitat. Anything you can provide for pollinators will give your little visitors the resources to skip on over to your next-door neighbor's house and visit their tomatoes. Or perhaps you shared your love for pollinators with your neighbors and they bought a few foxglove plants (*Digitalis* sp.), and even a few blueberry plants. Watch as the fuzzy little common eastern bumblebee draws nectar from your celosia and then flies across the yard to your neighbor's foxglove. She will continue to move throughout the neighborhood, flying up to two miles, to collect resources for her colony. Your small container garden may not look like a lot to you, but to her, it means the world.

There is no garden too small or landscape too large to include pollinator habitats. Together we can help protect our pollinator friends, and maybe we can inspire others along the way.

Index

Achillea spp. *See* yarrow

Agapostemon. See sweat bees

American Standard for Nursery Stock, 121

Ampulex canaliculata. See cockroach wasps

Ampulex ferruginea. See cockroach wasps

Ampulicidae. *See* cockroach wasps

Andrenidae. *See* mining bees

anemophily, 46–48

angiosperms, 5, 45–46

anise hyssop (*Agastache foeniculum*), 49, 144

Apiaceae. *See* parsley/carrot family

Apidae. *See* social bees

Asclepias spp. *See* milkweed

asters (*Symphyotrichum* spp.), 24, 41, 44, 53, 64, 66, 110, 139

azaleas (*Rhododendron* spp.), 42, 82

basil (*Ocimum basilicum*), 21, 31, 131, 137

basil bergamot (*Monarda clinopodia*), 145

beardtongue (*Penstemon digitalis*), 24, 49, 52

bee balm (*Monarda fistulosa*), 24, 104, 108, 139, 144

bee flies (family Bombyliidae), 20–21

bees (order Hymenoptera), 31–44. *See also specific kinds of bees*

beetles (order Coleoptera), 27–28

bird's-eye-view plan, 87

black-eyed Susans (*Rudbeckia* spp.), 6, 64, 66, 104, 108, 139, 144

bleeding heart (*Lamprocapnos spectabilis*), 64

blue hyssop (*Agastache* × 'Blue Fortune'), 56, 58, 69, 77

blue Sandhill lupine (*Lupinus diffusus*), 145

Bombus spp. *See* bumblebees

Bombyliidae. *See* bee flies

borage (*Borogo officinalis*), 134, 139

borage family (Boraginaceae), 52. *See also* borage

botanical gardens, 143, 145

bougainvillea (*Bougainvillea glabra*), 42

broadleaf pink purslane (*Portulaca amilis*), 145

Buddleia sp. *See* butterfly bush

bumblebees (*Bombus* spp.), 8, 12, 31–32, 35, 43–44, 62, 71, 145; common types of, 38; life cycle of, 35–37

butterflies (order Lepidoptera), 18, 22–27, 46, 48–51, 60, 62, 64, 67, 76, 135, 139, 145

butterfly bush (*Buddleia* sp.), 22, 24, 51, 118

butterfly weed (*Asclepsis tuberosa*), 26, 93, 95, 104, 108

buttonbush (*Cephalanthus occidentalis*), 82, 106

caffeine, 71

cardinal flower (*Lobelia cardinalis*), 56, 139

Carolina aster (*Ampelaster carolinus*), 85

carpenter bees (*Xylocopa* spp.), 36, 39, 51–52

celosia (*Celosia* spp.), 133, 139, 147

Chalcidoidea. *See* fig wasp

chervil (*Anthriscus cerefolium*), 49

cockroach wasps (family Ampulicidae), 30

Coleoptera. *See* beetles

colony collapse disorder (CCD), 10–11

columbine (*Aquilegia canadensis*), 24, 56, 120. *See also* eastern red columbine

comfrey (*Symphytum* spp.), 64–65, 76, 110

common yarrow (*Achillea millefollum*), 31

coneflowers (*Echinacea* spp.), 6, 24, 37, 41, 61–62, 67, 103. *See also* purple coneflowers container garden, 129–31

containerized plants, 118–21

corbicula, 48, 51–53. *See also* pollen basket

corpse flower (*Amorphophallus titanium*), 48

cosmos (*Cosmos bipinnatus*), 67, 120, 139

creeping snapdragon (*Asarina procumbens*), 130

creeping zinnia (*Sanvitalia procumbens*), 130

cuckoo bees, 43–44

dandelions (*Taraxacum officinale*), 51, 112

dead horse arum (*Helicodiceros muscivorous*), 22

devil strips. *See* parkways

digger bees, 10

dill (*Anetham graveolens*), 21, 24–25, 31, 49–50, 137

Diptera. *See* flies

direct sowing method, 119–20, 133

dogwood. *See* flowering dogwood

drones, 34–35

Dutchman's pipe (*Aristolochia macrophylla*), 22, 26

dwarf canna lilies (*Canna* spp.), 130

eastern cucurbit bee, 52

eastern honey bee (*Apis cerana*), 33

eastern prickly pear (*Opunita humifusa*), 49

eastern redbud (*Cersis canadensis*), 42, 82, 91, 106

eastern red columbine (*Aquilegia canadensis*), 104, 108

Echinacea spp. *See* coneflowers

elevation views, 87, 89, 98, 101

embedded pollinator habitats, 60

entomophily, 48

European honey bee. *See* western honey bee

evening primrose (*Oenothera drummondii*), 49, 51

Fabaceae. *See* pea family

false indigo (*Baptisia* spp.), 95, 102–4, 108

Farren, Bob, 145

fennel (*Foeniculum vulgare*), 21, 24, 31, 49–51, 137

fig (*Ficus carica*), 29

fig wasp (superfamily Chalcidoidea), 29

flies (order Diptera), 18–22

flowering apricot (*Prunus mume*), 1

flowering dogwood (*Cornus florida*), 22, 82

flowering maple (*Abutilon* spp.), 130

foodscaping, 137–39

forbs, 83

foxglove (*Digitalis* spp.), 147

fringe tree (*Chionanthus virginicus*), 82, 106

fuchsia (*Fuchsia* spp.), 64

furrow bees, 40, 54

garden bed preparation, 115–17

garden design: and color, 89; and formality, 57–58; and line and form, 89; and plant selection, 105; principles of, 96; qualities of, 101; and seasonality charts, 104

garden management, 123–27

garden planning, 78–81

garden renovation, 117

gentian sage (*Salvia patens* 'Patio Deep Blue'), 130

giant hyssop (*Agastache rupestris*), 73, 130

goat's beard (*Aruncus dioicus*), 44

golden Alexanders (*Zizia aurea*), 41, 49, 95, 105, 110

goldenrod (*Solidago* spp.), 24, 28, 38, 44, 49

golf courses, 145

great blue lobelia (*Lobelia siphilitica*), 49

Hadany, Lilach, 51

hardiness zones. *See* USDA hardiness zones

hawthorns (*Crataegus* spp.), 51, 70

Hitchmough, James, 10

honey bees, 31–35, 49, 51, 53–54, 60, 62, 67, 71, 77, 91, 93; and colony health, 10–12; and managed hives, 7–8, 10, 17–18; and stinging, 32, 34. *See also* western honey bee

Hoplitis spp., 52

hoverflies (family Syrphidae), 20

hummingbirds, 45, 49, 56, 62, 64, 147

Hymenoptera. *See* bees, wasps

hyssop, 29, 37, 77, 108. *See also* anise hyssop;
blue hyssop; giant hyssop

Indian blanket (*Gaillardia pulchella*), 145

irises (*Iris* spp.), 87

ironweed (*Veronina* spp.), 110, 139

Irwin, R., 71

Japanese maple (*Acer palmatum*), 118

Jekyll, Gertrude, 59–60

Joe-pye weed (*Eutrochium* spp. and *Eupatorium*
spp.), 86, 108, 144. *See also* spotted Joe-pye
weed; sweet Joe-pye weed

killer bees, 32

Kölreuter, Joseph Gottlieb, 7

lady's slipper orchids (*Cypripedium* spp.), 48–49

Langstroth hive, 8

Langstroth, L. L., 7–8

lantana (*Lantana camara*), 83, 130

lavender (*Lavandula augustifolia*), 30–31, 131

leafcutter bees (family Megachilidae), 39, 41–43,
51–52

lepidoptera, 22–24, 49, 62. *See also* butterflies;
moths

lobelia, 108. *See also* great blue lobelia

maiden pink (*Dianthus deltoides*), 23–24

mallow family (Malvaceae), 24

marigolds (*Tagetes erecta*), 31, 134, 137, 139

mason bees (*Osmia* spp.), 10, 43, 52

masses, 57, 59–60, 87, 89, 97, 103, 107. *See also*
sweeps

Megachilidae. *See* leafcutter bees

Mexican sunflowers (*Tithonia rotundifolia*), 24

milkweed (*Asclepias* spp.), 24, 26, 37, 120. *See also*
butterfly weed; purple milkweed; swamp
milkweed; tropical milkweed

mint (*Mentha* spp.), 24, 30, 147

mining bees (family Andrenidae), 41

moths, 22–23, 51, 56, 62, 67. *See also* lepidoptera

mountain mint (*Pycnanthemum* spp.), 76–77, 93,
95, 104, 108

myophiles, 20. *See also* bee flies; hoverflies

native bees, 2, 10, 13, 39, 41. *See also* solitary bees

neonicotinoids, 11–13, 120

ninebark (*Physocarpus* spp.), 68, 82–83, 106

North Carolina State University, 71, 73, 116, 140–43

oakleaf hydrangea (*Hydrangea quercifolia*), 22

Ophryocystis elektroscirrha, 27

oregano (*Origanum vulgare*), 30–31, 131, 134

parkways, 131–34

parsley (*Petroselinum crispum*), 24, 49, 137

parsley/carrot family (Apiaceae), 49–50, 67

partridge pea (*Chamaecrista fasciculata*), 145

passionflower vines (*Passiflora incarnata*),
24–25, 85

pea family (Fabaceae), 24, 52

phenological charts, 61–63

Pinehurst Resort, 145–46

pineweed (*Hypericum gentianoides*), 145

pink sedum (*Hylotelephium spectabile*), 58

pipevine swallowtail butterflies, 24, 26

planting techniques, 122

planting times, 121–22

plan view, 79, 98, 101. *See also* bird's-eye-view plan

pocket gardens, 134–35

poison hemlock (*Conium maculatum*), 49

pollen basket, 48, 52–54. *See also* corbicula

pollen brush. *See* scopa

purple coneflowers (*Echinacea purpurea*), 19, 24, 58, 63, 68, 70, 104, 108. *See also* coneflowers

purple milkweed (*Asclepsis purpurascens*), 26

purple salvia. *See* salvia

Queen Anne's lace (*Daucus carota*), 21, 24, 49

rain gardens, 139

rattlesnake master (*Eryngium yuccifolium*), 28, 31, 67, 93, 104, 108

red buckeye (*Aesculus pavia*), 56

redbud (*Cercis canadensis*), 42, 51, 69, 104. *See also* eastern redbud

red hot poker (*Kniphofia uvaria*), 58, 108

red maple (*Acer rubrum*), 82, 106

rosemary (*Salvia rosmarinus*), 31, 63, 104, 131

roses (*Rosa* spp.), 38, 42, 82

Rozanne hardy geranium (*Geranium* 'Rozanne'), 130

salvia (*Salvia* spp.), 36, 56–57, 110, 133

sapromyophiles, 20

saucer magnolia (*Magnolia × soulangeana*), 1, 28, 82

scopa, 53

sea lavender (*Limonium latifolium*), 31

sedum (*Sedum* spp.), 2, 66–67, 104, 110

shaggy fuzzyfoot bees, 10

Sherman, Rhonda, 116

skunk cabbage (*Symplocarpus foetidus*), 20, 22

snapdragon (*Antirrhinum majus*), 24

social bees (family Apidae), 31–33

solitary bees, 10, 32, 38–44, 49, 53–55

spicebush (*Lindera benzoin*), 24–25, 106

spicebush swallowtail butterflies, 24–25, 51

spotted Joe-pye weed (*Eutrochium maculatum*), 24

squash (*Cucurbita* spp.), 7–8, 35, 52, 134, 137

squash bees, 10, 52, 139

stand-alone pollinator habitats, 60

St. John's wort (*Hypericum perforatum*), 38–39, 49

sunflowers (*Helianthus annuus*), 18, 24, 41, 54, 71, 133–34, 139. *See also* Mexican sunflowers

swamp milkweed (*Asclepsis incarnata*), 26, 108

sweat bees (genus *Agapostemon*), 39–41, 145

sweeps, 59–60, 72. *See also* masses

sweet alyssum (*Alyssum maritimum*), 130, 147

sweet Joe-pye weed (*Eutrochium purpureum*), 139

Syrphidae. *See* hoverflies

tomatoes (*Solanum lycopersicum*), 8, 18, 35, 130, 134, 137, 139

tropical milkweed (*Asclepias curassavica*), 26–27

trumpet honeysuckle (*Lonicera sempervirens*), 49, 63, 104

U.S. Economic Research Service, 9

USDA hardiness zones, 2, 64, 83, 105–6

varied plantings, 60

wasps (order Hymenoptera), 20, 29–31. *See also* cockroach wasps

western honey bee (*Apis mellifera*), 7, 33, 34

Wilson, E. O., 44

Xerces Society for Invertebrate Conservation, 68–69

Xylocopa spp. *See* carpenter bees

yarrow (genus *Achillea*), 6, 21, 28, 44, 51. *See also* common yarrow

Yong, Ed, 30

yucca (*Yucca filamentosa*), 87, 89, 93, 105, 130, 133

zinnias (*Zinnia elegans*), 133